Cat
Sun Signs

Cat Sun Signs

Vivian Buchan

🅱

A SCARBOROUGH BOOK
STEIN AND DAY/*Publishers*/New York

FIRST SCARBOROUGH BOOKS EDITION 1983
Cat Sun Signs was originally published in hardcover by Stein and Day/*Publishers.*

Copyright © 1979 by Vivian Buchan
All rights reserved, Stein and Day, Incorporated
Designed by Louis Ditizio
Printed in the United States of America
Stein and Day/*Publishers*/Scarborough House,
Briarcliff Manor, N.Y. 10510

Library of Congress Cataloging in Publication Data

Buchan, Vivian.
    Cat sun signs.

    1. Astrology and pets. 2. Cats. I. Title.
BF1728.3.B82   133.5'8'6368   79-65117
ISBN 0-8128-6097-7

Contents

Beforeword   11

The *Aries* Cat (March 21 through April 20)   23

The *Taurus* Cat (April 21 through May 21)   33

The *Gemini* Cat (May 22 through June 21)   45

The *Cancer* Cat (June 22 through July 23)   55

The *Leo* Cat (July 24 through August 23)   67

The *Virgo* Cat (August 24 through September 23)   77

The *Libra* Cat (September 24 through October 23)   89

The *Scorpio* Cat (October 24 through November 22)   101

The *Sagittarius* Cat (November 23 through December 21)   113

The *Capricorn* Cat (December 22 through January 20)   125

The *Aquarius* Cat (January 21 through February 19)   137

The *Pisces* Cat (February 20 through March 20)   147

Afterword   155

This book is for
Duffy,   the Aries cat, who really is the
         Topcat he says he is,
Corky,   the Gemini cat, who upended the
         routine of two Taurus humans,
Susi,   the Taurus cat, who taught her charges
         how to boss those humans around,
Mitzi,   the Libra cat, who convinced humans
         that laps were for sitting on,
Neko,   the Pisces cat, who sleeps with the angels
         beneath a blue hydrangea bush in Cuernavaca,
         Mexico, his last resting place in this
         incarnation.

Cats do not merely demand civilization.
They create it.
—T.O. Beachcroft

Beforeword

By becoming acquainted with the characteristics of the twelve Sun signs, we can predict with 80 percent accuracy (sometimes more) how a person born in a certain Sun sign is going to react to us and to life in general. If we can do that with people, why can't we do it with our cats? Those predetermined traits are so uniquely distinctive that they can't be scrambled around to fit someone born under another Sun sign, and understanding those characteristics will give us an insight into why they react as they do. The sun is the most forceful of all the astral bodies, and it stamps us with a personality that goes with us through life. And it stamps our cats with personalities distinctly their own, for all creatures are affected by the electromagnetic vibrations emanating from the planets.

Let's remember we're not discussing horoscopes. Casting a horoscope is a complex study based on mathematical calculations of the aspects formed between a natal Sun and the position of the planets at the time of birth. This exact position is taken from a set of tables, known as an ephemeris, that has been carefully prepared by astronomers. And to determine this precise position requires an in-depth study by trained astrologers.

Furthermore, a horoscope is a prediction of what could happen in our lives when certain planets move into juxtaposition or opposition to other planets and how the vibrations generated at that time and place could affect an individual's destiny. And what self-respecting cat would pay the slightest attention to any prediction? It would be an exercise in futility to suggest to a cat that anyone (let alone a planet) could affect his environment or his ultimate destiny. His inviolate self-confidence and his elegant independence would reject such nonsense. He knows that tomorrow will hold for him exactly what he decides tomorrow shall hold. Nothing more, nothing less.

So out of respect for a cat's natural aversion to directives of any kind, we are going to consider only the planetary influences that were operating when he was born that made him what he indisputably is and always will be. But, of course, that astrological analysis will be a secret between you and me.

So, let's turn to astrology to gain a new insight into why our cats behave (or misbehave) as they do. For therein lies the key that will unlock at least one door to their complex and intriguing temperaments.

Granted that all cats are inquisitive, tenacious, independent, self-assured, and haughty, they do differ from one another in many ways. Let the ailurophobe who categorizes all cats as "just damned cats" explain the differences that we cat-controlled persons do know exist.

Let's ask him, for instance, why one cat will drink milk and another one abhors it; why one craves raw meat and another ignores it; why one is a homebody and another a gypsy; why one accepts cuddling and another rejects it; why one mopes and pouts and another laughs (even dances). Why is that cat jealous, this one neurotic, that one suspicious, this one shy?

Even after all the similarities and dissimilarities have been considered, there is one common denominator making all cats alike. And that is the aura of mystery that surrounds them. Sir Walter Scott, when he remarked to Washington Irving, "Ah, cats are a mysterious kind of folk," summed up the reason why people either hate or love cats.

It is that mystery that appeals to those who admire and respect cats and repulses those who see in that mystery something to be feared and avoided. To ailurophiles, a cat's mystery is what they cherish and respect; to ailurophobes, it is something ominous and threatening.

Ever since cats appeared on this planet, they have been either loved or despised. There is no middle ground. Nor is there any neutral ground, for that matter. In Ancient Egypt, they were worshiped; in the Holy Land, they were ignored; in Great Britain, they were tortured. Even though the cat has been an object of fear or downright hatred in the Western world until the last century, the cat has survived. It has done so with the aloof dignity that stems from his admirable confidence that he reigns supreme over man and circumstance.

Carl Van Vechten wrote in his book *Tiger in the House,* "It's the unconquerable spirit of the cat that has made it impossible for man to dominate, annihilate, or subjugate it to his whims and commands. The cat's supremacy over circumstances has kept it alive through centuries of torture, abuse, and hatred. And what man cannot control, he often fears."

Among the many hundreds of poets, essayists, and historians who have written about cats (one way or another) is Val Gielgud who is a playwright, broadcaster, producer, editor, and author. And an admirer of all kinds of cats. In his book, *Cats,* he wrote, "For a Beginning it might be better to go back to that statement of every childhood, which has about it something of the ring and certainty of the Commandments: THE CAT SAT ON THE MAT. He did. He does. He always will. We can go on from there."

And cats have gone from "there," which was first in Ancient Egypt when that civilization was flourishing circa 3100 B.C. It was during that period that the cat made its mysterious appearance from seemingly out of nowhere. However the cat got there, the Egyptians were fascinated with the creature. Its likeness was used on pilasters and frescoes, on shields and headdresses, and on jewelry and ornaments. Excavations in ancient cities have turned up exquisite statues of cats that indicate they were highly regarded and held in great esteem.

From Egypt the cat was transported to far-flung places by the seafaring Phoenicians who plied the sea lanes for commercial purposes. Eventually, the cat appeared "here," where, to all appearances, it intends to remain. But where the cat came from originally is subject to speculation, for it was part of civilization long before it was included in recorded history.

It behooves us to become better acquainted with the cat who's in charge of our household. Inasmuch as the various Sun signs harmonize more naturally with some and some are downright antagonistic to others, understanding why this is so may remove some of the confusion of why one person is disliked by a cat and another one can't keep cats from adoring him. Could it be that the person who can't keep a cat from flowing around his legs is astrologically in harmony with him? Could it be that I-don't-like-cats persons are so astrologically out of tune with the cats they've encountered by happenstance (never by choice, of course) that it makes them hate all cats?

When you discover why your Taurian cat is so obstinate while your sister's Cancer cat is so amenable, you will be more sympathetic with that aggravating stubborn streak Taurian cats are possessed with. And when you have learned why your Sagittarian cat wants to talk all the time, you will listen to him knowing that he has to talk simply because he has to.

And when you have arrived at that understanding, your cat is going to have a higher opinion of you and be more contented letting you live with him.

Millions of us will find that by better understanding our cats, living with them in our feline-managed domiciles will be far more pleasant than it has been. At the last census, it was learned that 35 percent of the households in the United States were under the supervisory paws of one or more cats.

And that means that 13 million homes have become king-doms ruled over by more than 36 million cats.

To understand the influence of the Sun signs on cats, I have not only consulted astrologers but observed the cats who have been indulgent enough to let me live with them and allowed me to cater to their whims. And I have listened to them talk. Talk? Of course. Cat language can be under-stood by anyone who is not deaf and who does not have a closed you-can't-convince-me type of mind.

Cat language is comprised of a large and colorful vocabu-lary. There are the purrs that are endless. The purr of wel-come, the purr of inquiry, the purr of satisfaction, the purr of affection, the purr of acceptance. Then there are the meows that express anger, pain, bewilderment, sadness, disgust, con-sternation, and impatience. One of the most appealing me-ows is the silent one where the mouth opens without sound coming out that means quiet pleading. Added to the purrs and meows is the vocabulary made up of squeals, howls, yowls, squalls, squeaks, shrieks. And every one of them means something different and expresses the varied emotions a cat feels and wants to talk about.

Start studying your cat's Sun sign to gain a greater insight into why your cat does or doesn't do what he does. Under-standing his temperament and personality is going to make him a lot happier and certainly give him a lot more respect for you after you come to your senses.

From now on, your cat will be referred to as "he," not because of feline chauvinism or sex discrimination but simply to avoid the he/she hassle we are all grappling with these days. Rest assured, however, that gender has little to do with his predetermined personality, which is bestowed upon your cat at birth through the powerful influence of the Sun.

Of course, there are all kinds of cats. There are dozens of breeds, sizes, and colors. There are indoor cats and outdoor cats. There are city cats and country cats. There are fat cats and lean cats. There are fluffy cats and sleek cats. There are gentlemen cats and lady cats. There are neutered cats and natural cats. But all of them are possessed of the felinity that makes them fascinating and challenging.

Now, there are some exceptions we need to consider. One is that a neutered cat is usually not as agressive nor as intense in its behavior as the non-neutered cat. It is true that neutered cats are more docile and muted than the natural cats who are permitted to sexualize with cats of the opposite sex. But the neutered cats will still exhibit their native traits even though they may be less demonstrative about doing it.

The second exception is that any native (human or otherwise) born on the cusp of his Sun sign will probably inherit some of the traits of the Sun sign adjacent to his own. To explain. When we talk about a cusp, we are referring to the last few days of a Sun sign or the first few days of that Sun sign.

For example. If your cat was born during the last few days of Taurus (say from May 19 to May 22), you may see some Gemini characteristics cropping up. If, on the other hand, your cat was born during the first days of Taurus (April 21 through April 23, let us say), you can expect to see some of the traits of the Aries native.

What this means is that your cat will still be predominantly Taurian in nature, but it will not be the dyed-in-the-wool Taurian that a cat born smack in the middle of this Sun sign would be.

I know some astrologers are going to protest this because they ignore the cusps as having any influence on the native. But there are others who do believe the cusps should be considered. And I belong to the latter group because I have observed this influence of the cusp not only on my own cats but on friends.

Another thing to remember is that we said we could predict with 80 percent accuracy (maybe more sometimes) how a native is going to behave because of his sun sign. This does not mean we can shoot for 100 percent accuracy.

No other stellar body has the power of the Sun, but other aspects such as the position of the Moon, the relationship of the planets to one another at the time of birth, and the degrees of movement the planets may have made at certain times of the day when the native was born all contribute to the overall personality.

But if we can predict with even 80 percent accuracy how our cat is going to behave and understand why it does what it does or does not do, it is a lot better than having no insight at all. Isn't it?

You are not going to be very successful changing your cat's predestined personality that he brought with him into this incarnation. You can be successful, however, in changing yourself and your attitude toward that enigmatic creature by viewing it through astrologically adjusted eyes.

And if that will make that feline lord and master who's in charge of your domain happier, then this book will have served its purpose.

Aries the Ram

(March 21 through April 20)

Let's get one thing straight
Here, now, and forevermore.
I'm the Topcat wherever I am and that
Includes this domicile.
Don't issue orders and expect me to obey them.
The only laws to be obeyed around here
Are the ones I issue.
As long as you understand that
We'll get along.
Harmony exists where there's only one boss.
And I'm it. Got that?

The *Aries* Cat

Even though he would deny it vigorously, an Aries cat is actually the infant of the whole zodiacal spectrum, for he was born in the first Sun sign—in the springtime of the zodiac. And like a baby, he is completely absorbed in himself and his feline world. He can't help believing the universe was created for him alone, for that is what his Sun sign ordained for him. So, naturally, what he wants to do and have will take priority over anything you want him to do and have. Make up your mind that he's the *boss* and that he's going to rule the roost— or else. And that else is something to be avoided.

Impetuous and impatient, he will ram through his nine lives, butting his way in and out of situations with supreme confidence that he is superior to anything or anyone. And the fact that he usually is only adds to his confidence. If he can't see a challenge advancing toward him, he goes out looking for one—even creating it if necessary. The neighborhood meanie (cat, boy, dog) will cross the street if he sees your cat and has tangled just once with him. Convinced that nothing can make his fur fly, your cat is oblivious to it when it does. Defeat is absolutely intolerable; so even when he is getting the worst of it, he plunges right back into a brawl determined that his adversary will go limping home. If he ever does take the brunt of a fight, he will nurse a grudge until he has settled the score. He will never forgive or forget the real or imagined insult or defeat until it has been properly dealt with and the score evened to his satisfaction.

Because he is volatile, emotional, and fiery, he goes up like a Roman candle the instant something agitates or aggravates him. But how can he help that? His ruling planet, Mars, not only endowed him with a pioneering spirit but set the pulsating blood of a warrior pounding through his veins. Natives of this Sun sign are natural protectors of turf and family. So let some snoopy stray wander through your yard and feel' that snarling hissing bundle of fury gripping his back just once. You will never see that cat again, for he will be halfway into the next county as soon as he can shake that lethal bundle of tooth and claw off his ripped-up back.

Like the ram that symbolizes Aries, he will butt his head against a closed door until it is booming with pain. It is his head that is going to catch the injuries when he gets into a fight. He'll come in from a night on the tiles nursing a ripped ear, a torn lip, or a swollen eye. Will that deter him from strutting right back the next night to settle the score? Foolish question.

It is his kittenlike faith in himself that keeps him from

24

learning from experience. As soon as something stops hurting, he has forgotten why it did and goes ramming back for more. He strides through the days with initiative, daring, and courage without taking time to consider the consequences until they slap him right on the end of his pugnacious nose.

Direct and uncomplicated, an Aries cat does not resort to sneakiness to get what he wants when you are not producing it quickly enough. His lungs are strong and powerful, and they are a part of his arsenal of weaponry. You would have to be deaf or wear earplugs if you expect to hold out against his insistent howling and yowling when he wants something right now.

He will yell, "Get that can of tuna open, will you, and make it snappy." And you will make it snappy. Don't expect him to sit quietly while you visit on the phone if he is hungry. And don't set anything before him he doesn't like, either. He is as apt to tip over the dish and scatter the food around the room as to walk away from it. A lashing tail and flashing eyes send the message, "That will teach you not to serve me that junk again."

You will learn within minutes after your Aries kitten swaggers into your home that you can't *tell* it to do anything that is opposed to what he wants to do. If you ask him politely, you may get cooperation. Then, again, you may not. But if it was something he intended to do anyway, he will be so amenable you will think you have gained authority at last. Disillusionment will follow very shortly.

If you ever see a cat strolling sedately along fastened to a leash, it won't be an Aries cat. No proud and superior creature like it would submit to such humiliation. "Just you try that, and I'll jerk my head off or chew the leash into shreds."

An Aries cat has the I.Q. of a Whiz Kid, and he will learn all he needs to know without help from you. Cats who learn the trick of turning a doorknob to get through a closed door are undoubtedly little Aries cats. Keep your yarn zipped into a knitting bag, all closet doors and dresser drawers closed. Better yet—lock them. For when your Aries cat wants in or out, he will manage it somehow. Furthermore, he is a mind reader. If he hears you *thinking* about taking him to the veterinarian for a distemper shot or a checkup, he will be doing a disappearing act. I am acquainted with an Aries cat who knows when his owner is just thinking about taking him to the veterinarian. She keeps the carrier in a closet with mops, brooms, a vacuum cleaner, etc. that she goes into several times every day. Just let her open the door to bring out the carrier, and the cat is off and running to a hiding place that takes the skill of a private eye to locate.

Although an Aries cat is difficult to discipline, it can be done. That is if you are willing to spend years—maybe a lifetime—and have the persistence of a Taurian. But he will never be coerced, cajoled, or commanded into becoming a sit-by-the-fire Cancer cat or a homeloving Taurus cat. It is not that he is downright disobedient; it is just that snoozing under a lilac bush or sitting on the front steps is a waste of time when there is so much to explore and stir into action. Snakes, bumblebees, butterflies, birds, chipmunks, your sewing basket, reading glasses, pan drawers, scraps of paper in a wastebasket—what are they all doing there if not to be played with or fought with?

But he is such a blithe, honest, excited little upstart that he is as irresistible as the baby he really is but doesn't know he is. And he is so loving and affectionate that when you have pleased him by your snap-to-attention deportment he will cream around your legs and even sit on your lap for five minutes letting you pet him.

Creatures born under Mars influence are not only fighters but lovers. Advances made by cats of the opposite sex are quickly and happily accepted. They are ready to engage in flirtations or affairs with either claimed or unclaimed lovers at the flick of a whisker. Your cat may very well be the most gossiped-about member of the feline circle in your area, which would not only tickle his fancy but be considered a badge of achievement. Your proud and fiery Martian is never going to settle for anything less than being Topcat throughout his empire.

Sitting on the porch watching traffic is not this cat's idea of living. It is simply ridiculous to waste time that way when there's so much out in the world to investigate.

Living with an Aries firecracker is a challenge (your cat will see to that), but it will never be dull. You will be proud of this gutsy, spunky feline even though you might complain to your friends that your Damned Cat drives you crazy.

COMPATIBLE SIGNS: Taurus, Leo, Libra, Sagittarius natives will not object to being bossed around by a fire-eater. In fact, they will find him more amusing than annoying and will not be overly concerned about what he does (or does not) do.

LESS-COMPATIBLE SIGNS: Pisces, Capricorn, Aquarius, Scorpio, Virgo, Cancer, Gemini natives will find it a harrowing

27

experience adapting to this cat unless they mend their ways and comply with his directives. When they do, they will find him an exciting and stimulating boss to work for and one they will come to enjoy even though jumping through hoops is part of the job.

NON-COMPATIBLE SIGN: Aries. Horrors! Until this native learns to control his own volatile temperament, he will have frequent and explosive clashes with his cat.

If you are an Aries, it will be your nervous system that collapses and your ulcers that begin quarreling with one another. It will not be your cat's nerves or ulcers that will be affected, for he would not tolerate giving in to such nonsense.

Of course, you could survive by using lots of patience and understanding with him, but rest assured he will not spend any thought on giving you any of either.

Taurus the Bull

(April 21 through May 21)

Of course I'm spoiled.
Spoiled rotten.
And why shouldn't I be?
I'm beautiful, elegant,
And cooperative (sometimes).
Only the best is good enough for
A treasure like me.
Don't buy second-class brands of food
For me. I won't touch it.
I expect the best of everything.
And that means thick cream and not that
Thin watered-down milk. And I want lots of
Everything.
Understand?

The *Taurus* Cat

Because he was born under the sign of the bull, you can't expect him to be any less stubborn than one. Taurus is a fixed earth sign, which means the natives are steady, practical, and dependable. But it also means they are persistent, unyielding, and obdurate creatures of habit. Although your Taurus cat does need care in handling, he is one of the most amicable cats you could belong to.

Taurus kittens are born mature and well-behaved; so they are less frisky and far more sensible than those born under some other Sun signs. Emotionally stable, a Taurus cat is not given to indulging in spells of depression or fits of pouting that keep you wondering if he is ill or angry. Nor is he given to euphoric bouts that cause you to wonder whether he's been tippling from the bourbon bottle.

When the day-to-day routine goes evenly along, your cat is

contented and placid. But let something happen to upset him or make him furious and his temper tantrums will be as explosive as a July 4th celebration. Like an enraged bull, he will storm around with flashing eyes and lashing tail, venting his fury until brave men seek cover under the coffee table or behind the water heater. Although his temper is quick to flare and violent while it lasts, it is just as quick to subside. And then he will look at you with reproachful eyes that say, "What on earth's the matter with you? You know very well it was all your fault that I got mad in the first place. You'd better be quick about apologizing, too, for I'm not going to take the blame for that episode." And that innocence isn't put on, either, for that is exactly what you did do—as far as he is concerned.

If you can persuade your little bullheaded cat to go the way you want him to go (and he is willing to go that way at the time), and you can get him to do the same thing for several days in a row, he will form a habit that endures. When a habit is fixed, it is fixed. And changing it can be as frustrating as trying to rearrange your concrete sidewalk with a coin-silver teaspoon.

Born under the influence of Venus, your cat could be referred to as the dimpled darling of the Universe if it were a two-legged creature instead of four. Venus endows Taurians with loving, affectionate, and amenable dispositions. That is if they are not goaded or pushed too hard or too often.

Peace loving and gentle by nature, your cat will not take kindly to shouted or yelled orders. He will turn on his paws, flounce out of earshot, and wait until you have calmed down and come to your senses. He is not defiant naturally; so instead of hissing or spitting, he will remove himself from your obnoxious presence. And regardless of what he has done or has not done that riled you, it is your fault. He will stare at you with unrelenting eyes, without uttering one meow, and glare, "You should know better than to yell at me. It just makes me more stubborn than I am. And that's mighty stubborn, as you'll find out."

As much as he covets peace, he craves comfort and luxury even more. Whatever provides a sensual pleasure is his cup of cream. He will adore sleeping in his own basket, snuggled into a soft woolly blanket (especially if it is fluffed over a heating pad in the winter). He will burrow under the covers on cold nights to snuggle up against you (particularly if your electric blanket is turned on). He will flop down on your lap or drape himself over your shoes with turtle-dove chortlings if you have filled his stomach with warm creamed kidney.

Taurians love to eat; so they are just as happy with hamburgers as they are with roast duckling. It is more a matter of quantity than a variety of epicurean rarities that pleases them. So your cat will croon over rich milk and broiled liver, but he will chomp his Friskies just as happily if that is what is set before him. Sturdy and strong (remember the bull?), he may run to paunchiness as he grows older. But his distended or sagging stomach will not concern him if that stomach is fully packed.

Inasmuch as he is a devoted-to-my-castle cat, he is not apt to be out prowling every night or wander far from his security blanket in the daytime. His heart is in his home, and he is not going to leave his heart very long. Because he is such a homebody, he is an impossible traveler. If you have not tried

35

taking him for a Sunday drive, don't. If you think you can overcome his rebellious behavior by attempting to get him adjusted to traveling, you will give up that idea after the first trial run. Just getting him to the veterinarian requires plotting as well as requisitioning help from a strong and fearless man.

Cats who sit on porches watching the world go by are undoubtedly Taurians, for they are peacefully contented just watching the bees and butterflies pursue their own fun without being tempted to join in. Your luxury-loving Venusian much prefers lounging on a velvet cushion in front of a crackling fire on a cold night to sneaking up and down dark alleys where belligerent cats might be spoiling for a fight. He will fight if he is forced to, but he will avoid a fight by walking around the block if he spies some bullycat swaggering down the avenue.

Your cat is not much of a socializer swapping yarns with the gossipers under the porch; so much of the scandal going on in the feline circles will not be known by this rather uncurious cat. To him, sniffing the pansies is just as enjoyable as listening to the latest carryings-on of the felines in the neighborhood.

He is not a whiz cat like an Aries or Gemini, but he is not a Mortimer Snerd, either. He is just a no-nonsense cat who reasons things out before he acts. "I'm not stoic or stodgy, I'm just cautious and deliberate," would be his evaluation of his intelligence. So do not be misled into believing he is incapable of thinking deeply on more than one level. When he sits with that out-to-lunch look on his face, he may be thinking thoughts that would astound the astronauts.

Once he has learned a lesson, he never forgets it. You will not catch this cat sticking a paw into that bush where a bee that was sitting on a peony blossom buzzed out and stung him.

Although he is sedate and mature, he is inventive about how he puts in his time. He is happy playing with a ball (a wad of aluminum foil does nicely, thank you), tossing a pipe cleaner in the air, pouncing on a chunk of yarn, or climbing the draperies. Just pray that he doesn't start clawing your new chair instead of his scratching post, for if he starts he will never stop.

Keep the stereo volume low and load the turntable with stacks of Mantovani records if you want him contented and peacefully stretched out on the sofa. He is so unable to stand racket and confusion that if he is forced to live with it he will become nervous and withdrawn. Screaming at him is useless; criticizing him is futile. He will disappear to the top shelf of a closet or crawl behind the bookcase and stay there until you come crawling on hands and knees to apologize.

Fundamentally, his affectionate disposition is so loving he will forgive you almost before you have asked him to. Some coaxing words and a bowl of Tender Vittles set in front of his hideyhole will tell him you are sorry to have been so lacking in proper conduct. Before long, he will stalk out with an air of injured dignity, almost ready to forgive you but certainly not to forget what you have done to insult him.

Taurus rules the heart and neck; so your cat will be susceptible to throat and chest disorders. Do not ignore spells of coughing or sneezing, for they are genuine. He is not given to putting on an act to get your attention, and he is more likely

to be ashamed of showing any weakness than displaying it. So
when he acts sick, he is sick. Bundle him into his carrier and
get him to the veterinarian even though his guttural moans
will sound as though you have slammed the car door on his
tail.

Because he is so enamored of pleasure and comfort, he is
going to be upset if you are sick or distressed. And he is so
intuitive he will sense it almost before you know there is
something wrong with yourself. He will lay a velvet paw
against your cheek to sympathize with you if you are nursing
a hangover. And he will snuggle against you if you are in bed
with the flu. Under the influence of Venus, he is endowed
with a loving heart that wants to both give and receive
affection.

Anything that upsets his routine will bother him exces-
sively. When he watches you packing a suitcase, he will look
so bereft that you may be tempted to forget that weekend
skiing trip, wondering if he will be able to survive without
you. It is wonderful to think that you will be so missed, but
keep in mind it may not be you that he is going to miss as
much as it will be the disruption in the routine you have
been trained to follow.

Living with a Taurus cat is rather pleasant, really, if you
put up a sign that says, "Don't ever try to drive him, for he
won't be driven. But he can be led." So fasten an invisible
rope (made of gentle words) to his collar, and tug it gently
from time to time to keep him going in the right direction. If
he doesn't know what's up, he will come trotting along behind you most of the time. He is bright enough to know that

if he keeps you happy most of the time you are going to be nicer to him all the time.

Wrap him up in a blanket of warmth and softness. Fill his ears with romantic music and his stomach with lots of food, and he will fill your home with peace and contentment.

COMPATIBLE SIGNS: Aries, Cancer, Leo, Libra, Scorpio, Capricorn, and Pisces natives have a natural affinity for Taurians. So in spite of personality differences, a native of any of these signs will be able to adjust quite willingly and effortlessly to the routine his home-loving and human-loving cat will establish for him to adhere to.

LESS-COMPATIBLE SIGNS: Virgo, Gemini, Sagittarius, Aquarius and Taurus natives are going to have a tough time handling this cat. But when you have come to the end of your rope and face up to the fact that your cat can hold out longer than you ever can, you will give in to him and maintain a semblance of peaceful coexistence.

Gemini the Twins

(May 22 through June 21)

Scram! Outa my way.
I'm in a hurry
To get where I'm going.
Do I know where that is?
Who wants to know?
Your foolish questions bore me
To distraction.
And I'm distracted enough
Without you constantly
Complaining about what
I'm doing. Knock it off,
Will ya?

The *Gemini* Cat

"In order to get where I'm going I have to run twice as fast," has been the modus operandi of your Gemini cat since he was able to stand up on his winged feet. Born under the influence of Mercury, he is a pulsating bundle of motion as difficult to pin down as a whiff of perfume or pick up as a drop of mercury. Holding a fistful of air is simple compared to holding a Mercurian cat.

He is here one minute, there the next, and nowhere the third. The drummer he hears plays a sixteen-beats-to-the-measure cadence, and your cat steps right in time to it. And you had better do the same if you are going to keep pace with him.

He is too impatient to wait for action to catch up with him, so he either chases it or creates it. You will not find him sitting in front of a hole watching for a mouse to come scampering out. Nor will he sit patiently in front of his empty bowl waiting for you to fill it with chow. He will howl his demand for quick service so that he can grab a fast bite and be on his way to wherever he thinks he's going. Even though he is not sure himself just where that is.

His mother probably believed she was giving birth to two litters of kittens at the same time when she ushered her June babies into this incarnation. And she was correct. Gemini is the sign of the twins; so those in this Sun sign have two distinct personalities and are motivated by dual desires that keep them changing directions without warning and becoming involved in several projects at once.

Then, too, this is an air sign, which means Gemini natives have quick, lively, and versatile minds to match their active bodies. Like the air, your cat wants to be everywhere at once. And it's remarkable how he almost achieves that goal. He is able to do two or more things at the same time without losing sight of the next thing he is planning to do. He may have one paw down in the fishbowl churning up a typhoon and giving the fish hysterics while he has one eye zeroed in on the bird cage estimating the leap that will knock it over and hopefully let the canary escape.

He is able to run from window to window following a squirrel's leap from tree to tree while he is tossing his catnip mouse in the air and catching it on the rebound. He is so alert he can hear an ant crawling across the patio floor and be able to pounce on it while he is chasing his marble across the bricks.

It is true that some cats covet routine, but they are not

Geminians. Schedules and routine are your cat's arch enemies. Confinement to him is worse than jail to a globetrotter. Trying to keep him shut in a room behind a closed door is as senseless as stuffing a mountain lion into a baby's highchair.

Of course, opening and shutting doors all day and night isn't easy to do without losing patience, but you will open and close them anyway. That is if you want to avoid being howled at and told, "Your attention to duty is expected. Your constant complaint that I'm on the wrong side of the door is utterly ridiculous. You're on the wrong side when I'm on the other. If I hear you say once more 'that damned cat wants out again' you're going to regret it. I'll see to that."

Depriving your freedom-loving cat of unrestricted and unlimited liberty will turn him into a drooping and sad little noncat and destroy the sparkling personality that makes him a fascinating and unpredictable cat, unlike any other.

Being creative and imaginative are inborn attributes; so you will need to keep his active mind occupied with plenty of playthings. Fill a basket with catnip mice, bells with bells inside, twisted pieces of wire, empty spools, pipe cleaners, strands of knotted yarn, and big marbles. He will paw out the one he wants, play with it for a few minutes, drop it, and trot back for another. Just remember as you go around the house and garden picking up his discarded toys that stooping is good for your waistline, if not for your disposition.

Some of your friends are going to lift their eyebrows and roll their eyes heavenward and ask, "What on earth is the matter with that cat? Is it hyperkinetic or just plain nuts?" If they do, explain nicely, "Of course not. He's a Gemini under the influence of Mercury, and his sign is the twins. What else can you expect?" Don't be overly concerned with what others think of your cat, for he is contented if you understand him. Who needs the approval of some dummy, anyway?

Although he is not a lap cat or a sit-by-the-fire feline, he is really very affectionate and will take time out to give you a quick slurp with his tongue on your hand or cheek (whichever is handier) as he races off to bank off the stair-wall while rushing down to check that funny noise in the furnace.

His range of vocalized sounds is almost as unlimited as his interest in action. And he loves to talk. His purrs, meows, growls, and howls make up a language you can understand if you listen hard enough. No other cat talks as much—except perhaps a Sagittarian—but chances are your cat would win a talkathon paws down pitted against the most talkative cat in the country. Encourage him to answer your questions and spend time answering his, and you will be surprised at what you will learn about what goes through a cat's head.

If the gods who created cats had seen fit to endow them with the ability to read and write, your Gemini intellectual would graduate magna cum laude from any Ivy League school and become another genius in any field that appealed to him.

Because he is less emotional than cats born under some Sun signs, he will not be as quick to show temper or retaliate He is a cool and rather private dude who is not exactly aloof but certainly not going to extremes to be admired and fawned over. Your cat will not be out prowling every night, either, looking for cats to fight with or make love to. It will take more than a challenging bully or an amorous flirt to deter this bundle of animation from where he is going—even though that destination may not be quite definite.

In spite of activity, your cat will be fastidious about his appearance; so he is slicked up and groomed to perfection all the time. Being persnickety about how he looks isn't all he is fussy about. He will demand that his litter pan be kept fresh and clean all the time. If there is anything that will fluff his ruff and turn him glassy-eyed with annoyance it is jumping into his pan and landing on something he deposited there that you neglected to remove.

Highstrung and nervous, expect him to jump three feet off the floor if you drop a skillet or someone comes roaring up the driveway on a motorcycle. You had better be careful, too, about turning on the vacuum cleaner unless you have explained your intentions, for that sudden racket will send him sliding around corners looking for a fast escape route to a hiding place.

His Sun sign presides over the chest, lungs, legs, and feet. So keep him warm and dry, for he is susceptible to pneumonia and chest colds. (Be sure to have that distemper shot needled into him every year.) Naturally, his inborn impulsiveness and inquisitiveness will make him accident prone. He is apt to pounce on a broken pop bottle mistaking it for a crouching chipmunk or take a fast wipe at a bumblebee believing it is a friendly fly. Then he will come yelping to find you full of dismay and distress, wondering what has gone wrong with his bleeding paw or his swelling lip.

Vibrant and dynamic though your winged cat was born to be, he is not always leaping and dashing around. Of course, he takes naps like all cats do. It is just that when he is awake

49

he displaces so much atmosphere it seems he is never in a state of suspension. It is the tug of two personalities in one little body that makes him captivating. Don't get the idea he is a schizophrenic. He is perfectly sane if a bit unbalanced.

Living with a Gemini cat is invigorating if you don't ask, "Why do you tear around like crazy? Where are you going now, for Pete's sake?" His answer to such sillies might be, "You can just tell Pete I don't know. I'm in a hurry to get there. Where's where? Who cares? Just gangway, will you?"

COMPATIBLE SIGNS: Gemini, Libra, Scorpio, Sagittarius, and Aquarian humans will be adored by a Gemini cat. You will make a mercurial twosome who will have fun living together. You are intuitive enough to know you can't fold fog into a wallet or bottle a whiff of perfume. So you won't even try to coerce your little winged creature—which suits him just fine.

LESS-COMPATIBLE SIGNS: Aries, Taurus, Cancer, Leo, Capricorn, Virgo, and Pisces natives will be overwhelmed and completely mystified by this whirlwind until they relax and let him fly around. Sooner or later, they will be trained to let him zoom into space to find that somewhere he is on his way to find—even if he does not know why he wants to find it.

Cancer the Crab

(June 22 through July 23)

Okay, so I fell off the couch.
What's so amusing about that?
You didn't have to laugh at me
And call everyone to come look.
You think I'm funny
When I'm being serious.
And then when I'm really cute
What do you do?
Scold me for being so silly.
I'm getting mighty baffled
By your unpredictable behavior.

The *Cancer* Cat

A kitten born under this Sun sign is a lunarbaby whose emotions will always be at the mercy of the moon's electromagnetic power even though it is 238,857 miles out there in space. As a result, when the moon moves through its synodic cycle, your cat's personality will undergo changes that might baffle you if you did not understand that astrologically he is unable to resist the tug of that silvery satellite.

He probably does not understand himself, either. Here he is moody and pensive this week when last week he was so carefree and giddy. Why is he so capricious one day and dreamy and broody the next? If you consulted the calendar to see when the moon is waxing or waning, you would have the answer and be able to predict when his moods would shift. Actually, it is more fascinating just to watch him yield to the moon's force.

It is easy to be misled into thinking a Cancer kitten is going to be a cinch to control because he is so gentle and docile. Behind that amicable front he is as determined and persistent as any cat you will ever encounter. Only he goes about getting what he wants in a quiet but insistent way and before you know it you have been manipulated and out-maneuvered. Because Cancer is a water sign, your cat will be more pliable and adaptable than cats born under the earth signs, but nonetheless he is still going to be in command of his environment and you.

His deck has five aces and he keeps them tucked into one mitten and knows exactly when to pull them out to take any trick he wants. His strategy is not going to be a direct, frontal attack, creating a head-on collision with you by howling and squalling for what he wants. His tactics are far more apt to win his battle with you, for he appeals to your love for him rather than forcing you to capitulate.

He will sit and look at you out of innocent, mournful eyes while he whimpers with soft meows that say, "You're neglecting me again, and I am sad." You may hold out for a half hour or so, but soon that insistent, gentle reprimand will become as unnerving as the howls of an impatient Aries cat who demands you stop what you are doing right here and now and cater to his demands.

Because he is patient by nature, he is also long-suffering and courteous most of the time. Even though he is starving for his dinner, he will sit silently in front of his empty dish until you have finished your telephone conversation or completed your typing. As soon as you place the receiver back on the cradle or tuck your letter into an envelope, he will set up his plaintive meowing telling you, "I'd like my supper now, please." He's not going to be like an Aries or Leo cat who throws himself against the refrigerator door howling with impatience because the milk he knows is in there isn't being served at his command. A Cancer cat knows the milk is in there, too, but he's more apt to pat the refrigerator with soft paws and rub his head against it purring for it to come out.

A moonkitten is so clownish and clumsy, you will spend hours laughing at him stumbling over his paws and making himself dizzy whirling around an empty bathtub trying to capture his tail. He loves being noticed and appreciated, but remember you have to laugh *with* him—not *at* him. When you do that, he will keep performing until he falls down in exhaustion.

The first months of a Cancer's kittenhood are extremely vital to his physical and emotional health for the rest of his life. If he is to develop into an affectionate and devoted cat, he will have to have love ladled over him by the barrelful. Keep in mind that the crab symbolizes this Sun sign and that in order for a crab to move forward it must go sideways. Your kitten can become so frustrated with obstacles or problems that could damage his self-confidence that he would crawfish his way through life. Cancerians who are neglected or abused when they are young grow into suspicious and distrusting adults. If you want a friendly, loving, openhearted cat give your crabkitten lots of attention and praise so it won't become a snarling, crabby old cat.

Because your moonbaby is so appealingly lovable, it will be hard to keep from spoiling it rotten. Actually, it does take a lot of balancing to walk that knife edge of pampering him enough and yet not making him revoltingly self-centered. But it is better to opt for an overindulged cat than a sad and withdrawn little neurotic. Pour love—lots of love—over the little imp and then settle back to enjoy the results.

A lunarbaby should never be teased or roughed up. He is too sensitive and shy to tolerate the emotional or physical strain of being tormented or pummeled. And he is so super-sensitive to criticism that if his feelings are bruised, he may crawl into the hammock he made by tearing a hole in the bottom of the boxspring cover and mope there for hours nursing his injured feelings. It may take you hours on your hands and knees to convince him that he misunderstood you or that you didn't really mean what you said or did.

Dealing with a sensitive soul requires a handle-with-white-gloves approach to keep from accidentally hurting his tender feelings. If he jumps on your lap when you are reading the newspaper and you push him down, he is going to feel horri-bly rejected. And if you unconsciously push him out of bed when he is sleeping on your feet, he will slink away wonder-ing what he did to make you so mad at him.

Animals do cry real tears when they are in pain or feel abused; so if you ever see a cat with tears dripping off its whiskers, it will be a Cancer cat, for no other Sun sign brings on such sudden and copious floods of tears as this one.

Understanding your mooncat is not all that difficult, how-ever, if you keep reminding yourself that he is going to experience sudden shifts in mood without warning or reason. If he stops right in the middle of a romp with his rubber mouse and sits in the middle of the floor with a far-off, not-with-it look in his eyes, it may simply mean he has just caught strains of celestial music floating down from the moon. Or it could be that he suddenly remembered something you did yesterday that upset him. Or it may be that he thought you were laughing at him and not with him when he was chasing his tail. It is nothing to worry about, however, for he can't escape being responsive to the unseen vibrations that make him so emotional.

Your cat has a long, long memory that he refers to when he needs a guideline for his own conduct. Reaching down into his storehouse of memories is what makes him sympathetic and compassionate when you are sick with a miserable cold or battling the Monday blahs. He will find the memory of the night you took him to bed a year ago after he had fallen downstairs and hurt his leg. Or he will find the memory of the time when you got up every two hours for ten days to give him the night-time medication he needed for his bronchitis. So he will refer to such memories when he wants to let you know he cares that you are suffering.

He may leap into your lap and lay his head against your arm and purr soft condolences against your ear. Or he may push up against your leg and look up at you with sympathetic eyes that say, "I'm sorry you have to go to work on mornings when you've got the blues."

Moonlit nights when other felines are slinking along the grass stalking their shadows or another cat, your moonbaby will be sitting in the window enraptured with the silvery moonshine flooding over him. He will be watching the shadows on the carpet as he cocks one ear to catch the greetings of the man in the moon. He will be too entranced even to notice a seductive kitten promenading under the window or too enchanted with the moonbeams even to hear the caterwauling of two cats engaged in making war or love.

When the moon is in one phase, he may be in such a moonstruck mood that you will secretly wonder whether you are living with a loony creature. Then, again when he is in one of his fantasies, he will be so quiet and meditative you will think he is an uncat. But these moods are what make your cat so intriguing you will emphatically defend him if some person says, "What a crazy-mixed-up cat!"

Don't let such an unfair statement go unanswered, for it amounts to defamation of character. Answer thusly, "I wouldn't trade my sensitive and mystical cat for any other cat on earth—or on the moon, or any other planet."

Inasmuch as a Cancer cat is susceptible to coughs, bronchitis, kidney disorders, or stomach upsets, you are going to have to be alert to detect any unusual behavior. Your cat will try to ignore any discomfort, hoping it will go away; so he will not groan or moan to get your attention. He will just try in his usual gentle but persistent fashion to get the message across. Even though he knows a trip to the doctor may result, he is too smart to let that deter him. Kidney disorders require immediate attention; so if he teases you to follow him to the litter pan, he may be trying to show you he has a real problem that requires medical treatment.

If you want a stay-by-your-side cat who will remain loyal and devoted all the days of his life, use the keys of kindness and love to unlock the door to his loving and gentle heart. Depriving him of your devotion will cause his moonlit soul to droop like a white violet under a hot noonday sun. He is too sensitive to survive even in the protected world you provide if he is not wrapped in silver moonglow and his delicate spirit tucked into a blanket of kind understanding.

If you will spoil him and ooze through his paws like melted butter, he will stay with you through thick and thin, prosperity and poverty, health and sickness for as long as he lives.

COMPATIBLE SIGNS: Cancer. You will have a love affair going from the first instant you lay eyes on one another. Your own home-loving tendencies and your own gentle disposition will harmonize from the beginning without effort. You will understand that both of you are moonstruck, so you will bear with him when the moon affects his moods. And he will bear with you when the moon turns you into a daffydilly, too.

LESS-COMPATIBLE SIGNS: An Aries, Gemini, Virgo, Libra, or Aquarius native will have to expend effort to understand the sometimes dreamy, sometimes loony, sometimes not-with-it Cancer cat. On the other hand, a Taurus, Leo, Scorpio, Pisces or Capricorn human will not be too overwhelmed by this mooncat because you are tolerant and willing to adapt yourself to your cat. If you bestow plenty of love on him, life with a Cancer cat could be as delightful as strolling in the moonlight with a sweetheart.

NON-COMPATIBLE SIGN: Sagittarius. No way! The one possibility is to buy a prayer rug and kneel before the zodiac three times a day beseeching the gods for guidance.

It will require persistent effort on your part to keep you

from driving this cat into a mean and cranky old crab. Your personality is too overwhelming for him unless you can tone down your direct and often critical comments.

Home to this cat is a haven while to you it is a place to toss your hat for the few minutes you will be there. The stability your cat needs to become the loving and devoted cat he was ordained to be would be hard for you to supply.

Leo the Lion

(July 24 through August 23)

Who's an egomaniac? Not me.
I'm just the best
Damned cat on this planet.
Probably in the universe.
Where would you ever find another
Specimen of feline gorgeousness like me?
You wouldn't.
There's none could even come close.
When it comes to style and class,
I'd be the Best of Show anywhere.

The *Leo* Cat

Born beneath the blazing golden-summer sun in the fire sign of Leo (symbolized by the lion), your little royal fluff mounted the throne the moment kitten legs could walk. Refusing to serve an apprenticeship as a monarch-in-training, he began surveying his empire with a possessive eye long before he was able to lash his tail or knew how to roar.

Vain, indolent, beautiful, splendid, magnificent, arrogant, intelligent! Put "super" in front of those adjectives and you'll have a portrait of your lioncat. There's something about the way he enters a room that reveals his high-born regality. His arrogant walk and condescending expression make you feel dowdy and unkempt even when you're in your best clothes. You stand up a bit taller, suck in your stomach, and rearrange your mussed-up hair. And if you're sensitive to disapproval, you may slink off to spruce up a bit before returning to your majesty's presence.

From the first moment the kitten opened his eyes, he was determined that under no circumstances would he ever—ever—ever be ignored. Just try it. No, better not. His immediate retaliation would be to emit such roars the neighbors would come running to your aid. But they, too, would cower before the flashing eyes and lashing tail of an outraged escapee from some jungle. And if that wasn't enough, sparks from upstanding fur would.

Your lioncat was born ordained to be a ruler; so he began practicing his technique and strategy when he was a toddler. By the time a kitten is grown up, he'll have his tactics refined to an art. Underneath all that bluster and bravado, though, is a little pussycat who yearns to love and be loved more than anything else in the world. Well, almost, for he craves attention and admiration almost as much as affection.

He will purr like a boiling teakettle when he is fawned over, praised, and patted. So, although his roars may sound ferocious, they are really more noise than substance. Mostly he roars because he loves being dramatic and front stage center with all spotlights focused on him. Even so, he is not all that sure he is as brave as he roars he is. Meeting the challenges of maintaining a kingdom requires an outward show of authority if he is going to keep control of his monarchy.

Although your fire-breathing Leo cat will indulge in sudden temper tantrums (violent while they last), they are usually as brief as spring showers—especially if you ignore him. Soon he will come flowing around your legs wanting to regain your attention and approval.

Because Leos are born to be leaders, your cat can't help

expecting every creature (including humans) to follow meekly along behind him. Any cat foolish enough to challenge this lion's superiority is not going to forget that encounter of the worst kind. Your cat will fight to the finish— lick off his paws, smooth down his rumpled fur and stride arrogantly away leaving his battered adversary without a backward glance.

He will march down the avenue completely unconcerned about what he has done to his victim. Does a king sympathize with an underling who has just had his head lopped off for defying him?

From the day he was born he will play, eat, sleep, walk, and make love with royal dignity. Until the day he dies, he will retain that regality. And his life will be a long one, too, for he has the strength and vitality of a lion as well as the wisdom to conserve his energy. Like his jungle cousin, a Leo cat is not going to exert himself anymore than is absolutely necessary. Why should he? You are there to do the exerting for him, aren't you?

So when your cat stretches out before a crackling fire expecting you to carry his bowl of food in to him, you had better be certain he can hear you operating the electric can opener and getting his favorite foods set out on his silver platter. While you're at it, better polish it.

He won't whimper, wheedle, sneak, or connive to keep you firmly pinned beneath his paws. And he won't spend time cultivating his higher-than-average intelligence. He won't need to. He will learn just enough to keep you submissive and subservient. His attitude is, "Why should I learn to turn a doorknob when I want to go out or come in, and why should I struggle to drag that silly mouse out from under the sofa when you're there to do it for me?" His arrogance is enough to keep you cowed and behaving as a well-trained servant waiting on royalty.

Determined to have admiration and attention, he will be the star of every performance—yours or his. You will not find him cowering behind the washer or cringing behind the shower curtain when your party is in full swing. He will be sitting right in the middle of the room surrounded by your admiring guests whose ohs and ahs are music to his ears and pats to his ego.

Strangely enough (well, not so strangely at that), a Leo cat makes a doting and devoted parent. Why not? What could be more delightful than sitting in the center of a circle of round-eyed kittens giving their undivided attention to the lessons an experienced and successful monarch is teaching them. As long as parent-cat has their undivided and breathless attention, they can roll, tumble, crawl all over the nice big soft thing, which makes them happy kittens adoring their lord and master.

You will despair of ever taming your tyrant. And you will fail horribly, too, unless you begin disciplining from the first day he takes your home into his custody. You will never accomplish it through sternness, punishment, or scolding. The more force you apply, the more resistance you will encounter. The louder you yell, the louder he will roar. The only way to open that defiant heart is to turn the lock with a key of love. And you had better keep that lock well oiled with plenty of attention, too.

Anytime you encounter a Leo cat who snarls, hisses, or

70

bites, you are meeting one who was a starved-for-love and neglected kitten. If he is deprived of love when he is little, his self-confidence will not only be jeopardized by the secret fear that he is not all that much of a lion as he roars that he is but he will lose faith in his supreme self-assurance.

His sublime ego can't be suppressed, coerced, or neglected for long without an explosion sooner or later. Just watch a lion in the zoo pacing savagely back and forth in his cage, and consider what would happen if you unlatched the door. That will give you an inkling of what a Leo kitten can grow into if he is not handled with delicate care and given lots of doting attention.

Freedom is an obsession with this domestic cat just as it is with a jungle cat, so don't expect to tame this creature into a lap-sitting cat, like a Taurus or Cancer cat. Spare yourself the anguish of seeing your screens punctured or your curtains slashed to ribbons by jumping to open or close doors when your orders are issued to you.

He craves attention and adulation so much that you probably can't provide all that is desired. So your cat will always be on the prowl searching for responsive and promiscuous partners who are ready to engage in sexual encounters with little prompting.

This sign rules over the heart, so you can expect to be confronted with high fevers or perhaps circulatory problems if your cat gets sick. Accidents will result from cuts or burns with the legs suffering more abuse than the body or head. Even though he may feel like yowling with pain, his supreme faith in his superiority over his environment will keep him from admitting that he is in trouble. Sudden illnesses can't be trifled with. Keep in mind that with his intense and sensitive temperament, everything that happens to him will be intense.

Living with a Leo cat is comparable to sitting on a keg of dynamite with a lighted fuse racing toward it. But life will never be dull. It will be vivid drama from dawn to dawn. And it will be exhilarating if you understand that this firecracker is a True Aristrocrat. To nurture that need-to-be-loved explosive but secretly melted-butter-inside cat, pick him up several times a day and whisper he's Mr. Gorgeous, watch him play, and praise him for his grace and agility. Pamper him when he behaves; ignore him (if you can) when he misbehaves. And life will be more or less pleasant if you bow to the supremacy of your lioncat and serve him faithfully.

COMPATIBLE SIGNS: Aries, Taurus, Cancer, Virgo, Libra, Scorpio, Sagittarius, and Aquarius humans have a natural affinity for a Leo cat—strange as it seems. If one of these signs is yours, you will have little trouble arriving at the agreement that the cat is the king and you are the serf. And, happily, all of you will enjoy your cat—and he will enjoy you.

LESS-COMPATIBLE SIGNS: A Leo, Gemini, Capricorn, or Pisces native will need to study his cat's Sun sign as well as be willing to sublimate his own inclinations to preen his ego to the preening of his cat's. If you are a native of these Sun signs, you can harmonize with a Leocat if you post a sign that says: "I will tell my cat I love him. I will pay attention to him. I will let him rule the whole house and environs."

NON-COMPATIBLE SIGN: Capricorn. Impossible!

Virgo the Virgin

(August 24 through September 23)

I'm not going through that door today.
Can't you see it's raining
And there are puddles
Everywhere?
Why should I dirty my feet
When I'm the one who has
To lick them clean.
You wouldn't like to lick
Your dirty feet with your tongue,
Would you?
So don't ask me to do something
You wouldn't do.
What do you take me for?
A dummy?

The *Virgo* Cat

No matter how long your Virgo cat lives, he will always have an innocence and naïveté about him that is enchanting. Virgo, symbolized by the virgin, indicates chastity, not that it can be taken literally by either humans or cats, but it does signify that proper conduct and conventional attitudes are very important to a Virgonian.

Because your virgin feline is so trusting and ingenuous, you could be deluded into thinking he is easily coerced and managed. Right? Wrong. Even though he is vulnerable, he is not going to be taken advantage of, for he is still a cat with the fundamental feline belief in his preordained superiority over his environment.

There is no question, though, that a virgin kitten is more obedient than most cats, but don't be deluded into thinking he does not know how to train you to be obedient. Not only can he train you, but he will do it so quickly and effortlessly that before you suspect what has happened you will be firmly pinned beneath his paws. Perhaps it is because he is so solemn and sedate that he appears harmless and guileless. But that is only a mask that covers a determined mind behind a deceptively innocent face.

A Virgo kitten is so anxious to do the proper thing that even when he is hardly able to climb over the side of his litter pan, he will claw his way to the top even though he knows he will fall flat on his nose on the other side, face down in the litter. It would be unthinkable for him to decide that climbing into that pan was too big a chore and opt for the handy flower pot because it was easier to get into.

As soon as he learns his tongue can be used for something other than lapping milk, he begins using it as a washcloth for his entire body. A Virgo cat can be so vain that no one should be surprised to see him standing in front of a full-length mirror turning first one way and then another to assure himself that he is as beautiful as he knows he is. Every hair must be slicked into place, every toenail clean, and every paw pad spotless. He would rather face up to a snarling Doberman than walk through a mud puddle.

He is not only so fastidious that he becomes almost insufferable, but he is a stickler for routine and order. He will be upset if his dish is moved one inch from where he expects it to be or if his basket is moved to another room or even another corner. And if his blanket is taken away to be washed, he will be distraught even though he would be more distraught if it was not.

Although he is not as stubborn as a Taurus cat, he will be

obstinate when it comes to his routine. He is determined that everything proceed according to his time clock which is always accurate all day—every day. He wants his milk and Friskies not only served right on the dot but placed exactly on the same dot every meal. Those mornings you plan to sleep late will be as difficult for you as for him. But it will be a rare morning that he does not see to it that his breakfast is served on his schedule—not yours.

Oh, he will not howl or stomp around raising a ruckus. He will sit on your chest gazing at you pitifully as he makes poor-little-me whimperings that eventually get you on your feet and staggering into the kitchen to prepare his usual breakfast. You can probably do it half asleep, for he wants the same thing every morning. When you discover what that is, don't try switching brands or even flavors on him. And don't let the supply run out, either. Flouting your duty is something not easily forgiven. Any lack of efficiency on your part or inattentiveness to his wishes will incur his vocally expressed displeasure.

Although a Virgo cat may appear delicate and slight, he has a wiry and strong body with surprising strength and resiliency. Intelligence and sensitivity are stamped all over his face, and his eyes are so luminous you can almost see your reflection in them. He is a smart cat, too, with lots going for him in the intellectual department. But he is smart enough to know that brains aren't all that important when it comes to manipulating you. It is the quiet, persistent and calm determination that gets that job done—not an IQ.

There is something almost angelic about this cat. He is so collected, dutiful, and dependable he does not seem to possess the felinity of other cats. But that lovely soul can become cranky and irritable if he is frustrated.

His nervous system is easily set askew (by the way, do you know cats and humans have almost identical nervous systems?); so he will suffer from indigestion and stomach disorders if he is put under too much stress. He would be a hypochrondriac if he knew about that malady, for he is a worrier. Especially about his health. It is not too difficult as a rule to determine when most cats are ailing, for most of them learn to announce their distress. With your Virgo cat, however, you may need a refresher course in ESP or clairvoyance to know whether he is really getting sick or just putting on an act to get your attention.

He is apt to resort to mournful whimpering if he thinks he is being ignored, just to make you think he is getting sick so that you will snap to attention. And yet he could be sicker than you suspect, for he is so sensitive that if the fish you gave him last night smelled just a bit queer, he could get sick from sniffing at it. Don't worry about him ever getting food poisoning, however, for he would growl at off-color food and storm, "Get that sickening stuff out of my sight and serve me something decent."

Even though a virgin cat appears aloof and self-assured, he still needs more love than he lets on. Although he will never be a show-off like a Leo cat or a whirlwind like a Gemini, he wants to be noticed and appreciated. He probably won't burrow under the covers to sleep on your stomach or curl up on your lap purring gratefully, for such behavior might rumple his fur or muss up his whiskers. He is more concerned with keeping himself unruffled than getting mussed up crawling over you to show his affection. Although he is prudent and conservative about displaying his devotion (as he is about everything else), it does not mean he won't feel as much love for you as the most amorous kitten on this planet.

Because he displaces so little atmosphere, it would be possible to keep him in an apartment where pets are forbidden for months (even years) without the landlord or even the neighbors knowing you were harboring a forbidden delight. The doorbell would be enough to send him racing for a hideyhole, which is where he will cringe until whoever came in goes out. And he is so reticent that even your friends will rarely see much of him. The can't-stand-cats folk will never see him at all. (He knows by their vibrations before they ring the doorbell.) They may catch a glimpse of something flying through the air and mistake it for a shadow or a piece of lint. But they would have no idea it was a real live threat to their sanity.

Unlike felines that go tromping up and down dark streets looking for excitement or mystery, your cat will not be a bit enthusiastic about that pastime. When he is out sizing up what is going on in the cat world, he will unintentionally attract the attention of sexpots even when he is not trying to or interested. It may be that the cool and self-contained bearing makes cats of the opposite sex feel that they are in the presence of an unattainable sexy creature.

Because this sign is an earth sign, your cat won't be the firecracker who is always casting an eye toward come-hither invitations. A Virgo's natural inclination to keep his impeccableness unimpaired will make sexual encounters less appealing. But, of course, he is no celibate, either. After all, he *is* a cat, for heaven's sake. But he will be fastidious about whom he does accept for a night's rendezvous.

Now, if you think he has no major flaws in his character, you are mistaken. Hasten to apprize yourself of one ever-present trait that may drive you to drink. He is critical! And living with a critical and faultfinding creature (be it human or animal) is a tough assignment. Your cat is so ultracritical about the way you conduct yourself that it takes skill not to veer to the right when he thinks you should be going left. As long as you walk his chalk line, or what he considers to be proper, and keep his household running like a well-oiled and perfectly adjusted machine, he will tolerate you. But if you are a slapdash housekeeper doing your chores when the spirit moves you, his criticism will be vociferously expressed.

If you forget that his breakfast is to be served at 7 A.M. sharp in his own sterile dish in exactly the right spot, or if you forget that today is the day his blanket goes into the washer, or you keep him up too late when you are having a party, you will drive him up the wall. Literally. He is apt to crawl under the blankets on the top shelf of the linen closet and collapse with a nervous breakdown.

Unlike a Cancer cat who is sympathetic when you are sick, your virgin cat is not going to disintegrate over the condition of your health. He may disintegrate, all right, but only because you are upsetting his routine. Don't expect him to crawl into bed with you and croon sympathetically in your ear. He is more apt to stand at the foot of the bed and squall, "I'm being neglected, and I'm not one bit happy about it. Get out of that bed and attend to your duties, which are me."

The *Virgo* Cat

Actually, a Virgo cat is something like the persnickity old maid in a cartoon strip who is finicky as well as critical about her neighbors. But, even so, there is something so beguiling about his innocence, his candor, and his serious-mindedness that he charms those who understand him.

COMPATIBLE SIGNS: Leo, Scorpio, Capricorn. Somehow these natives are able to survive under a Virgo's critical eye and be able to keep from collapsing as they meet their virgin cat's demands for law, order, and proper behavior.

NON-COMPATIBLE SIGNS: All the others. Unless, that is, natives of these signs make the effort to adjust their lifestyle to suit their cat. It is certain that he is not going to change, so you will have to—unless you want to break his heart or find yourself making reservations for a padded cell.

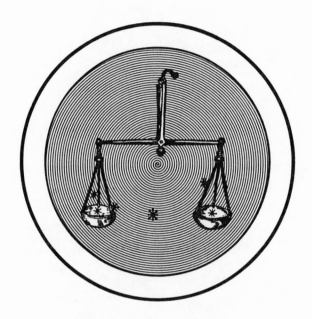

Libra the Scales

(September 24 through October 23)

This has been a horrible day.
And it's all your fault.
You got cross when I wanted to go out
And then decided I didn't want to
Go after all.
And you yelled at me to make up my mind
About taking a nap.
You kept shouting all day.
"Hurry up, get down, come here, go there,
Go to bed, don't dawdle, eat your chow."
Why can't you just leave me
Alone when I'm trying to decide
What I want to do? I don't care what you want me to
   do
Anyway. When you frustrate me even more
Than I am normally frustrated,
I am really frustrated.

The *Libra* Cat

If you have ever tried to keep a delicate set of scales in perfect balance, you can sympathize with your Libra cat. And you may need to reserve some sympathy for yourself if you don't understand the problems your cat has to cope with.

Under the influence of Venus with the scales of perfect justice as the symbol of this Sun sign, your cat is not only emotional but as changeable in his moods as moire taffeta (or a Cancer cat). When the gods parcel out the personality traits of this Sun sign, they toss in a mixture that makes a complex package of the native. But, thanks to the feline godmother who looks after kittens, your cat is one of the most loving and lovable creatures of any in any other Sun sign.

Venus endows her creatures with a winsomeness and love-ableness that add up to charisma. Some of that attraction lies in their appearance, so unlike the pixie faces of most cats, a scaleskitten's face resembles a fluffy pink powder puff or a giant strawberry bonbon. Of course, Libra kittens come in all colors, sizes, and breeds, but they all have a sugar-cookie appearance they never lose. A Libra kitten is so adorable that it's hard to keep from squeezing it unconscious. On the other hand, it can be so contrary and aggravating that you may regret not having followed your first inclination.

One side of a Libra's scales is heaped high with sweetness, goodness, and charm; the other side is piled high with desires for vigorous and lusty activity. And it takes serious concentration to keep the sides in balance; so it does not happen very often. But when the scales are in alignment, it is divine living with a Libra cat. It is then that he is comparable to a flower-bedecked fairy dancing in the moonlight. One flower too many, though, and then the scales tilt. And there you are dealing with a moody cat who is no longer a fairy but a borderline devil. Just a twitch of his whiskers or a sudden outburst from you can upset that delicate counterpoise.

One day he may be cooperative, the next obstinate (make that from one hour to the next). Some days he will be so contrary that you will entertain thoughts of tossing him to that cat-hating mongrel across the street. You are late for a meeting, and he refuses to come into the house; you are planning to sleep late New Year's Day, and he is peeved because you stayed up so late. He will demand that you get up and serve his breakfast at 6 A.M. to punish you. You have prepared his dinner, [creamed kidney] and he sits staring out the window with his back toward you (one ear cocked in your direction to hear your pleadings) but refusing to listen to your entreaties to come and get it while it's warm.

It is not contrariness altogether that creates a problem for both of you. It is his indecisiveness and inability to make a choice without weighing all the pros and cons, the frontward and backward, of any conclusion. He circles the idea or problem with the same wary caution he would if he was confronted with a strange cat who had strayed onto his turf.

Unlike the Gemini with the dual personality, a Libra cat does not have two sides to his nature. He is just a victim of the extreme emotions that keep him vacillating. Choosing between two alternatives keeps him teetering on the fulcrum, reluctant to move to the right or left. And heaven help him if there are more than two alternatives to consider.

Sometimes when he sits like a ceramic cat without blinking an eyelash, he may be wondering, "Now, should I sit in the window and wait for that white kitten next door to come out for her sunbath, or should I mosey out to the kitchen for that snack I heard being put down for me?" Or, "Is it better to take my nap now and then go looking for bumblebees, or should I go out now and play before taking my nap?"

It may take some time to reach a decision, but when it is reached a team of Percherons could not budge him—unless, of course, something tips his scales, and he is confronted with another emotion luring him in another direction.

Highly emotional and susceptible to stimuli, he does not do anything halfway even though he may sense his scales are tipping precariously. When he plays or prowls, he will be so enthusiastic that he will keep at it until he is completely pooped. Then he will stagger to his basket and be barely strong enough to lift a paw or struggle to his food dish. Those days he will expect you to either carry the food to him or him to it.

A Libra is sometimes considered lazy—but lazy he is not. It is just that whatever he does, he does to extremes. And when he is exhausted, he is so exhausted that he can't twitch the end of his tail or flick a single whisker.

Smart as any cat has a right to be, your cat is so deliberate making up his mind that he appears retarded at times. But he is bright enough. He can't help it if trying to arrive at a decision keeps him immobilized with a "I'm-not-in-here" look in his eyes that makes him look vacant.

So never give him a choice of anything. It will drive you to desperation and him to disintegration. Serve his food one dish at a time. Put down his cat chow, he will chomp it down. Put down his milk, he will lap it up. Put down his liver, he will lick the platter clean. Put them in a row, and he will sit there mesmerized wondering which one to begin eating—and probably not eating any of it.

You will learn never to give him a catnip mouse and a pipe cleaner to play with at the same time. Throw out his mouse— wham—he pounces on it. But don't toss out the pipe cleaner until you have hidden the mouse, or he will sit looking at first one and then the other and never get around to playing with either of them.

Because he is more freedom loving than some cats, he will want plenty of it inside and outside the house. He will be as ardent and passionate as are all natives of Venus; so he loves to love and be loved. But if two attractive felines sashay by at the same time, he will become so disorganized wondering which one to choose, he will ponder, "Should I go after that white one who looks so angelic or that slinky, tawny creature who looks sexy and willing?" He may waver so long weighing the charms of one against the other that both of them wander off.

Of course, all these momentous decisions are a drain on his vitality and strength; so there will be days when he is barely able to stand up. And you will wonder, of course, if he is sick. He probably is not. He is just restoring his strength to continue his should-I-shouldn't-I deliberations. Call to him then, and he may turn up that valentine face with a pleading look that says, "Please, don't annoy me today. I'm totally done in, and I need time to recharge my batteries." On the other hand, he could just as easily growl with indignation, "You've disrupted my reveries, so I'm going to remove myself from your irksome presence and sleep in the clothes basket if I can drag my weary self that far."

The constant push-pull on his emotions acts, of course, on the nervous system; it is imperative that you keep his environment as tranquil and serene as possible so that he will have that stability and security to lean on. Loud noises, blaring music, raucous voices, late parties can bring on nervous indigestion. And if he is exposed to such racket for too long a time he can collapse with a complete nervous breakdown.

He is highly susceptible to kidney and liver disorders; so be alert for urinary infections or bladder blockages. He is not so brave that he will slink into a dark corner to suffer in silence. He will be scared enough to make every effort to tell you something just does not feel quite right.

He will be upset when you are, for he is so sensitive he can pick up your moods. Possessed by that innate desire to see that justice always asserts itself (remember the scales?), he is going to be distressed if he thinks you have been treated unfairly. So if you are in traction with a broken leg or in bed with a 104-degree temperature, he will begin his deliberations. They'll go something like this:

"Now, should I get on the bed and purr my sympathy, or should I slip quietly away?" Or, "I hesitate to insist on my supper tonight, but I am very hungry. What should I do? Set up a howl for attention or go sit by my empty dish and starve to death?"

Your cat needs more than harmony and tranquility. He needs time (lots of it) to pursue his own interests and deliberations without your impatient demands to come to a decision and get on with this or that, which will only upset his equilibrium. It is quite enough for him to cope with his tilting scales without your adding criticism that could tip them out of balance. If you keep in mind that any decision he finally reaches will be the right one for him at that moment, you will be tolerant of the time it takes him to reach that conclusion. Let him ride up and down on his emotional yo-yo, for he can't help doing it. He will learn to handle his vacillations if you leave him alone—and don't expect him to make snap decisions about anything.

The *Libra* Cat

COMPATIBLE SIGNS: A Libra native will have a made-in-heaven relationship with a Libra cat. It will be a love affair from Day One. Aries, Taurus, Gemini, Leo, Scorpio, Capricorn, and Aquarius natives can harmonize quite easily with a Libra cat. You can "make the scene" together without too much effort on either side and become a very contented twosome.

LESS-COMPATIBLE SIGNS: The Cancer, Virgo, Pisces, or Sagittarius human is going to find the going somewhat tough until he understands what makes a Libra cat do what he does and then is patient with the push-pull tug that keeps a Libra cat off balance more than on.

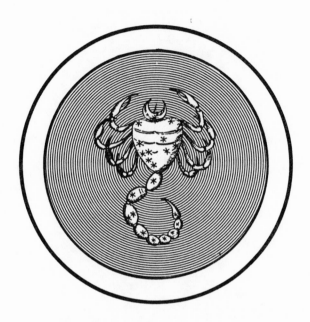

Scorpio the Scorpion

(Eagle or Gray Lizard)
(October 24 through November 22)

Let's have no more discussion
About last night.
Just because I stayed out until 3 A.M.
Is no reason for all this commotion.
Why was I so late?
What concern of yours is that?
My business at night
Is my business.
I don't ask you what you do all night,
So don't ask me.
Let's get that straightened out
Once and for all.

The *Scorpio* Cat

Born in a water sign under the planetary vibrations of Pluto, your cat is a combination of emotions that can make him difficult to understand—let alone handle. And you will have trouble unless you understand why a Scorpio native behaves as he does. The living with your complex cat can be fun *if* you respect the predetermined personality traits he brought with him when he entered this plane of action.

On the surface, your cat appears calm and cool like a quiet, stream of water; underneath, there is a bundle of complex emotions heated to the boiling point. Add to those emotions a determination as strong as a piece of tempered steel honed to a razor-sharp edge, and you will have a reasonably accurate description of a Scorpio cat.

Endowed with a gigantic ego and excessive pride, this cat believes he can accomplish anything he sets out to do and

 101

emerge victorious from any encounter. As a kitten, your cat sprang full-blown into this world with a body as strong as the determination that controls it. From the first day he takes charge of his domain, he has just one command he expects you to obey. "Now hear this. There's just one master in this place. And I'm it! We'll have no more insubordination."

If you are a gentle, soft-spoken, and tender-hearted soul, you will be firmly pinned beneath steely paws that will bear down on you with the power of a V-8 engine. He is going to need strict discipline from the first day (which will be bitterly resented) or you will be lapping milk from his saucer while he sits in your swivel rocker drinking coffee from your mug. And you will be scrunched down in his basket while he luxuriates full length on your quilted bedspread.

Do his velvety purrs and low-pitched, melodious meows mean he is complying with your requests? Funny, funny you. That beguiling exterior is a foil to protect a determined heart and mind that are working full time conniving ways to outwit you.

If your cat is typical of natives of this Sun sign, he has heavy or sharp features with a more-than-usual pointed nose and a luxuriant coat that is silky and lush. It will be the eyes, though, that will be so hypnotic that you will be under a spell without knowing how or when you got there. If you look deeply into them, however, you will see those burning emotions that keep him forever pushing onward and upward. Unlike cats with open and beguiling faces on which their emotions are candidly expressed, your scorpioncat's face wears an expression of lofty indifference. Hah! Indifference? Not a chance. He is so engrossed in analyzing you and estimating your reactions to him that he feigns lack of interest to keep you off balance. It is not that he is wicked or sly, but he is not innocent or naive, either. He believes he can unravel you, and when he does he will be able to roll you into a neat ball that he can push around as he pleases.

It's the influence of the mysterious planet, Pluto, that instills in a Scorpio native the desire to probe the innermost secrets of another's mind. Strange as it seems, a Scorpio cat does seem to have an inordinate amount of ESP. If you are wise, you will go into another room (close the door) to do your thinking.

His mountain-high and ocean-deep ego will never tolerate an insult or an injury to his pride or dignity. He will get his revenge sooner or later—one way or another. He will not leap at you with laid-back ears or snarl at you if you have insulted him. He will stalk off to his own private place and begin plotting his revenge.

He may wait until he hears you backing the car out of the garage and then streak for that new velvet chair and begin tearing at it with tooth and claw. Or he may wait until you are talking on the phone and then knock a bottle of imported perfume off your dressing table and stand gloating over it as the stuff oozes into the shag carpet. Or he may bat your reading glasses into the basement and stuff them behind the furnace.

You can be sure that if you bump into his ego, he will retaliate in some way no matter how long it takes. And his memory is verrrrry long when it comes to an affront to his pride. If some cat bests him in a battle, and he slinks home with a torn ear, he will never give up until he corners that foolish foe and challenges him to another fight. Your cat will eventually send that cocky cat home yowling [with two torn ears—if he has any ears left at all.] Your cat will not only teach him a lesson but pound the whole subject of proper respect for a Scorpio cat into the battered head. His victim will learn more about a scorpioncat than he ever wanted to know.

Your cat's M.O. is: Don't take an ear for an ear. Take two ears for one.

There will be days when you will be uneasy wondering just what is making him so placid and subdued. Those will be the days you will let your carelessness keep you from closing the closet door or pushing the dresser drawer clear shut. If you are that foolish, do not be surprised when you fnd your garment bags torn open and your prized cashmere sweater wadded into a ball in the bottom of his basket. Or that all the Kleenex has been pulled out of the box and torn into confetti. Or that all the neckties are piled under the bed.

It is not that he is being naughty. It is just that his burning interest in mystery fills him with uncontrollable urges to see what is inside, under, over, behind, on top of everything. If your cat could read, he would sit for hours immersed in whodunits and lug home a stack of detective magazines from the library every week. That's why a high shelf, a closed door, a clothes hamper are such challenges that they simply have to be explored. So keep your precious belongings and dangerous substances under lock and key. Carry the key in your pocket or around your neck.

Endowed with strength and vitality, your cat will resist sickness with stoic indifference and lofty unconcern. He simply can't comprehend that anything could overpower him; so he will fight off pain until he is in real danger. With his passion to overcome, when he does get sick he is going to be desperately sick because he will refuse to give in. Courageous and uncomplaining, he will slink away to suffer in silence without making a bid for attention. It may require the deductive powers of a supersleuth to determine what is wrong with him in time to get him to a doctor before it is too late.

Paradoxically, when you are sick he flips up the other side of the coin. A Scorpio cat is not only analytical but intuitive; you will hear him purring beside you as he brushes your feverish face with his eyelashes, if you are smitten with the miseries. And he won't take kindly, either, to anything that threatens your safety. Fiercely loyal and aggressive, he would attack an intruder so violently he would think a wildcat was evening the score. And you will never have to worry that someone will alienate your cat's affections, for he is not going to be taken in by anyone oohhing and aahhing over him, even though his ego would be inflated by the attention.

He would be the one to discover a fire in the wastebasket and come howling to tell you the house was on fire. (He would have called the fire department first, if he could dial the phone).

He is a champion of the undercat who might be taking a pummeling in some fight. And your cat would jump right into the middle of the fray and drive the bullycat back to his own turf. And if you think some little kitten who trots up to your cat's dish of liver is going to get swatted across the room, think again. Your cat would politely step aside and graciously invite the little visitor to help himself.

105

When a Scorpio cat moves into the neighborhood, the feline population passes the good word along. It is not long before the newcomer is besieged with propositions, but there will never be so many that a Scorpio cat can't handle them all, because no other cat (except perhaps an Aries) can hold a candle to your cat's 300-watt passion. Even a Leo's ardor would dim in the presence of a Scorpio native (be it human or animal). The seething emotions roiling within that bundle of complexity are not all confined to controlling his domain and the humans in it. A good many of them are dedicated to intense lovemaking. So cats of the opposite sex are always going to be caterwauling under the window of a Scorpio cat.

Just when you have despaired of ever curtailing his fierce determination to be Topcat everywhere, he will become so sweet and submissive that you will melt like whipped cream all over him. It's then that you will be ashamed, thinking you have misjudged him. Foolish One. Just remind yourself that underneath that deceptively beguiling facade is some overriding plan to emerge triumphant over something or someone—probably you. He is merely evaluating the angles that will be the most successful.

So when your Pluto-influenced cat sets out to rule you and his domain, acquiesce gracefully. You might as well, for you will have to sooner or later. Recognizing him for the superb creature he truly is will make it easier for you to let him be King of the Mountain. Regardless of how many times he faces defeat or humiliation, like the Phoenix that symbolizes Pluto, your cat will rise from the ashes of defeat triumphantly.

This sign is by far the strongest and most intense sign of

all. There is nothing wishy-washy about a Scorpio. The weakness (?) lies in the desire to go to extremes in all things. Like the pendulum of a clock that is set into such violent motion that it bangs the sides of the case, your cat's pendulum of emotions is going to be swinging wildly most of the time.

If you don't want a morbid or moody cat who borders on being psychopathic, don't try to break his indomitable spirit. You can't do it. But you can drive your cat to the last outpost of neuroticism if you haven't the good sense to let him alone.

Born in the tawny autumn when the countryside is a blaze of vibrant color, your cat is a vivid creature with blazing emotions that were implanted in him at birth.

His tremendous faith in his superiority is not a figment of his imagination. He really *is* superior. He is spectacular because he is a combination of flash and fire. Cherish it.

COMPATIBLE SIGNS: Taurus, Cancer, and Libra natives should have little trouble adjusting to a Scorpio cat. The loving natures of these humans appeals to a scorpioncat. That is not to say you won't face a challenge, but you should be able to cope without collapsing.

LESS-COMPATIBLE SIGNS: All the others with the exception of Scorpio. Until natives of those Sun signs can respect that label "Handle With Utmost Care" and understand that Pluto has endowed Scorpio natives with most unusual and unique characteristics, there will be conflict. When they come to their senses, coexistence should become possible—perhaps even pleasant.

 107

NON-COMPATIBLE SIGN: Scorpio. It is possible that these two combustible creatures could eventually exist in an armed-truce arrangement, each of them with a white flag over the head. But it will take time and patience on your part to adapt to a creature much like yourself. When you can flatter his ego instead of your own, life should become endurable.

Sagittarius the Archer

(November 22 through December 22)

No, I won't shut up.
I like to talk.
And I intend to talk
All I please, where I please,
When I please.
If you'd listen to me talk
You'd be a lot smarter than you are now.
It's a pity you can't realize
How much knowledge I have about so
Many things.
I can only make a few different sounds,
But, oh boy, can I make those sounds take on
Meaning. You'd learn a lot from me if you'd
Just shut up and listen.

The *Sagittarius* Cat

No matter how big your archercat becomes on the outside, he will remain a kitten inside all his life. From Day First to Day Last, he will be the happy little clown with a sunshiny heart who will bubble over with animation and joy. Born under the influence of Jupiter in the fire sign of Sagittarius, symbolized by the archer with bow and arrow, your little centaurian will be a happy-go-lucky, blithe spirit who will endear himself to you forever.

There is nothing he delights more in than expressing his affection and having affection poured all over him. When your friends drop in for coffee and neglect to pat his up-turned beaming face, he will leave the room with a hurting heart. Friendly and outgoing, he likes and trusts everybody. Nothing pleases him more than being right in the middle of the action. Move his basket into the party room where he can

 113

listen to the music and laughter, and he will drop off to sleep in the middle of his purrs of contentment.

You are not only his security blanket but his sun, moon, and stars. Without your freely given love, he will grow into a sad little drooping bundle of dejection sitting in a corner gazing mournfully at the wall. If you shower him with affection, however, he will give you a hundred laughs a day.

A clumsy and awkward little clown, his antics amuse you even when they aggravate you. The old adage, "A cat always lands on its feet" (not necessarily true), does not apply to this cat. Unlike most cats who move with the grace and litheness of a Nijinsky, your cat will stumble over his own paws as well as your feet, fall off a shelf or table, or miss landing on the window sill by inches. But with a happy confidence in himself, he will pick himself up and try again without a trace of embarrassment or humiliation.

Endowed with the insatiable curiosity of all felines, this little centaur has more of it than he can handle. He *must* know what is in every drawer, behind every door, and inside of every sack and carton. And he will never give up until he finds out, even if he knocks down a flower pot or has to tear open a gift-wrapped package in his search for the answer.

Sagittarians love to talk, even though they say the wrong thing at the wrong time for the wrong reason. And they never seem to know when enough is enough; so they keep getting in deeper and deeper with every word.

If you learn your cat's language (and you can), you will be asked incessant questions that demand quick answers. "Why

114

do bumblebees sting me and kiss the flowers?" "Where do I go when I go to sleep?" "Why do leaves fall down and not up?" "Is a firefly a lost star?"

Is it inborn curiosity that creates such wonderment or the levels of intelligence his mind operates on? Ask him. He will tell you.

The archer drawing his bow and sending an arrow into the bull's-eye right on dead center characterizes the directness and lack of duplicity of a Sagittarian. Completely honest himself, he expects honesty in return. So be wary of trying to deceive your cat, for he can spot a falsehood as accurately as a Geiger counter can detect radiation.

Here is a cat who will never stoop to sneakiness to outwit you, for there is not a deceptive whisker on his face or a dishonest thought in his mind. And if he catches you lying to him, he will never forget or forgive. If he is standing on the floor screaming for that last slice of liverwurst he knows is on the counter and you tell him it is for your sandwich or the dog's lunch, it had jolly well better be. He will stand right there until he sees either you or the dog eating it; so be sure one of you does.

Once he has caught you telling him an untruth, he will hold it against you from then on until he departs for Cat Heaven. So don't say, "Come on, fella, we're going for a nice jaunt in the country [Sagittarians love to travel], which will be fun," and then deposit him on the veterinarian's examining table.

It is far wiser to walk right up to him, look him straight in the eye, and say, "Okay, Tommy old boy, it's time for your distemper shot. We're off to the clinic, so hop into your carrier. I know you despise that rotten needle, but you've got to take it. So, let's go!"

Although his ear-rupturing groans and heart-rending moans will fill the car with every turn of the wheels, at least you have been honest with him (you can wear earplugs) and earned his respect.

Freedom is as necessary to this feline as it is to born-free Elsa; so confining him too much to the premises is an error in judgment. Freedom he needs—freedom he must have. And freedom he will get—one way or the other. Home to a Sagittarian cat is only a place to eat and sleep, certainly not the sanctuary it is to a Taurus or Cancer cat.

Unlike the Virgo cat who expects his domain to be kept in meticulous order, your cat won't care a hoot what happens in the housekeeping department even if nothing happens. He takes a devil-may-care attitude toward bedmaking and window washing (a bunch of nonsense, anyway); so don't worry if none of it gets done. Unless it is bugging you, it is a cinch it won't be bugging him.

The yeast will begin rising while he is still growing out of kittenhood, and he will be howling at the moon long before he has been told about the procedures of mating. He will know all about such things before most cats know there's an opposite sex.

Born in a fire sign, your little archer can't help being impetuous, and he can't tolerate being tied to apron strings. To keep that happy grin on his face, let him come and go at will. He is trustworthy enough to check in for meals. And he will be so eager to report what he has been up to he won't stay away from home too long. It may take some time to tell you what he has stirred up out there (you'll get over blushing in time), for you can be sure he did not spend those dark and magical hours sleeping under some honeysuckle bush.

He is exasperating at times, for unlike cats who can wind themselves around knicknacks without touching a one, your cat will be knocking them over like bowling pins—not because he sets out to do that, you understand, but because he can't control his unpredictable movements. Like the archer, he zeroes in on his target and moves straight toward it, no matter what's in the way. And what he can't understand is why you wring your hands over a vase lying in splinters on the floor when it made such a lovely tinkling sound when it fell off the table.

If felines organized themselves into service clubs instead of prides, they would probably organize one to aid all undercats. And it would be called Cat Vista or Feline Philanthropists. And your cat, if he didn't organize the club, would be the first volunteer. A champion of the downtrodden, he is the cat who will leap into the middle of a brawl if some squealing little kitten (or puppy) is being tormented and molested by some bully (boy, cat, dog). He is too in love with everything alive to be a killer; so don't expect him to be a mouser or a big eradicator. He is much more apt to play with a mouse than clobber it to death. The poor thing would probably die of fright from the playful batting around it gets, but it would not die from a crunched neck. A spider or a beetle might collapse from running away from your cat, but if it runs long enough it would be safe because your cat's not interested in ending the life of anything.

Born to be friendly, he simply can't understand unfriendly people. If some cat-disliker shies away from your cat's advances by tucking his or her legs under the chair to keep from going home with furry pants or hose with runs, your little centaurcat will be confused. "I like you. Why don't you like me?" will be written all over his bewildered face.

He does not understand rejection; so he never expects it. He will push his nose close to a snake under a bush expecting it to respond nicely to his "Hi, how are you today?" and then fall back in dismay when it hisses at him. He will take a swipe at a bumblebee and then sit licking a stinging paw with a betrayed expression on his face.

Because he is determined to solve every puzzle he encounters, he blunders into accidents. He will come home with cut paws, lacerated ears, and torn claws—not so much from fighting, but from poking his inquisitive nose, ears, and eyes into every curious thing. He is less apt to fall victim to organic disorders; so keeping him healthy does not require too much knowledge of internal feline disorders.

Your happy little clown will keep his sunny disposition until the Big Cat in the Sky calls him to explore another region, and he will undoubtedly be the same blithe spirit up there as he is here. Your centaur will be a sunbeam all the days of this incarnation if you shower him with affection and give him the freedom he must have in order to wander through the intriguing places he finds without much effort.

COMPATIBLE SIGNS: An Aries, Gemini, Leo, Libra, or Aquarius human will blend easily and harmoniously with the Sagittarian feline. Living with your merry little madcap will be

118

delightful, for your home and your heart will be filled with the sunshine this happy soul provides.

LESS-COMPATIBLE SIGNS: A Taurus, Cancer, Virgo, Capricorn, Scorpio, or Pisces native will have to make some major adjustments in his deportment and attitudes if he is going to keep this cat sane and sunny. You view your home as something to be cherished and stayed in. And it will aggravate you that your cat does not feel the same way about his home.

NON-COMPATIBLE SIGN: Sagittarius. On the surface, it would seem this native would get along with his cat beautifully because of their mutual attitudes toward life and home. The trouble arises because the human is out of the home more than he is in it, and the feline who wants the human there to listen to his escapades is not going to have an ear to talk into. And that is going to keep the cat very unsettled and quite unhappy.

119

Capricorn the Goat

(December 22 through January 20)

That scruffy looking cat's
Been hanging around here again.
Does he think I'd stoop to buddy
Around with him? Whew!
He even smells bad when he's down wind.
I'll just mosey on over there
And send that Skid-Row candidate packing.
I'll sidle up real friendly like
And then . . . POW! I'll let him have it
Right on the nose.
He won't be lurking around here
After I give him what for.
He's lowering the respectability
Of this neighborhood.
And he's got to go.
So here I go. . . .

The *Capricorn* Cat

There's a strange aspect about this Sun sign that makes a native resemble a little withered-up man when he is born and a virile stripling youth when he's old. It has something to do with the old year moving off stage and the new one entering from the wings.

Capricorn kittens are born looking mature, with serious expressions on their faces. Usually they pass right through kittenhood without pausing to engage in kittenish behavior. Under the influence of Saturn, they are astrologically predisposed to be moody, gloomy, withdrawn, broody. This planet gives Capricorns dispositions that can become surly and sullen at worst but never jovial and lighthearted at best.

Symbolized by the goat, the Sun sign gives patience and persistence to get to the top; so your cat will plod steadily and sturdily to attain the top position in your household.

 125

It may take some time for you to find out just what is going on though, for you can be easily deceived. You think, "My goodness, he's so dependable, timid and nonaggressive. And he's so obedient and amiable, he can't really be power mad." Upside that is the way he appears; downside he is as tough as any alley cat who has fought for survival since birth. But that is your cat's most guarded secret, for therein lies his power over you and his environment.

Make no mistake about it. Your goatcat will control you and your (his?) home without making waves or throwing temper fits to do it. Without twitching one whisker to right or left, he will move like a mountain goat toward his goal, with his eyes focused straight ahead, totally dedicated to getting to where he wants to go. He won't defy you; so when you issue a directive he will just sit staring at you without blinking an eyelash or flicking one inch of his tail. Is he agreeing? Disagreeing? Well—will he, won't he? You will not find out until he has decided, but in the meantime he will not reveal a single thought of what is going on behind that inscrutable face. If he does not intend to comply with your wishes, he will wait until you have forgotten about it or decided that forcing him to do it is not worth the effort. Passive resistance is his forte.

From the first, goatkittens take themselves so seriously they begin studying cat etiquette. They watch Mama with wide respectful eyes as she teaches them to wash their faces, climb into the litter box, usurp the softest chair, and eat only what pleases them. They learn precisely how to get what they want without creating uncatlike commotion. Perhaps it is because they are such sobersides when they are young and

126

held down by Mama's supervisory paws that when they do escape they begin kicking up their paws like the kittens they never were able to be. But no matter how kittenish they may become in their senior-citizen era, they never lose their dignity.

This peculiar reversal in feline maturation makes Capricorn kittens extremely vulnerable to illnesses when they are young while at the same time they build up a greater resistance to ailments that overtake mature cats. All the disorders that beset small kittens should be viewed with caution and the proper inoculations provided, for Capricorn kittens become sick more often and more seriously than those born under other planetary influences.

Solemn and serious, the Capricorn kitten looks upon baby talk and cuddling as something foolish and frivolous. He is so pompous at times that he makes humans feel downright giddy and flighty if they want to play with him. Leaping for that strand of yarn, bouncing on a wad of paper, crawling into empty sacks, pawing through the pan drawer are things a Capricorn kitten would consider downright ridiculous and a waste of time or energy. Furthermore, how do such silly pastimes advance the intellect?

Mapping out the day's activities requires concentration; so your cat may not sleep as much as most cats. If you could see into his mind, you would be astonished at the deliberate layout he is planning. "Now when shall I take my bath, manicure my nails on the scratching post, play to get some exercise, take a turn around the garden to check on whether the weeding, was done?" After he has planned his day, he will follow through without a change in plans. No sudden reversals or impulsive sorties into the next street will distract this proper cat from his appointed plans.

Unlike the Aries pulsating with impulsiveness, always seeking (or creating) excitement, your cat will avoid it. And like the Taurus cat, he will stay close to home, for he wants to know that security blanket is securely at his back. He will be more content staying with you, checking your attention to his routine, and sleeping in his nice clean basket, than climbing in and out of garbage cans or strolling along strange alleys.

Undutiful or undependable behavior on your part simply will not be tolerated. So don't go dashing out for a day of sleuthing through antique shops without cleaning his litter box and setting his food down in the proper place in the proper dishes. And don't expect him to crawl into a bed with bedding that is not washed at least once a week or lick up meals that are spasmodically and indifferently prepared.

After he has selected his favorite chair, do not make the mistake of sitting down in it when he wants to be there. He will not snarl or hiss at you, but he will stand in front of you glaring at you until you become so uncomfortable you move to another chair and apologize to him while you are doing it.

His rules of etiquette make it imperative that another's comfort is observed, which, of course, applies only to your respect for his comfort and has nothing whatsoever to do with his respect for your comfort.

Highstrung people make him nervous, for he is too self-regimented to relate to harum-scarums. People who toss down the newspaper and shout, "Hey, let's take in that new movie at the Bijou tonight," make him resentful because they upset him. He will not adapt to sudden spurts of house-cleaning either. Tell him today that tomorrow is the day the curtains get washed and the mop and vacuum cleaner are coming out for action. Then he can spend the night studying how to cope with that disruption.

Routine is so essential to his idea of proper conduct that you will rue the day you do not provide it. He will wait until you leave for the supermarket and sharpen his claws on the sofa. Then he may drag out your knitting and rip out several rows of an intricate pattern. Or he could decide to tip all the books out of the bookcase and carry some of them to the basement.

If felines had a social register, your Capricorn cat would never rest until he was listed among the Four Hundred. If he does not have a pedigree from a distinguished line of blue-ribbon winners, he simply assumes his papers were misplaced by some careless registrar. If he does have a pedigree, he will expect it to be framed in gold leaf and displayed in the foyer.

No matter how luxurious your home may be, he would prefer it to be even more so. If he can sit on the front steps of a prestigious home, he will nod patronizingly to less fortunate felines enviously eyeing him but refuse to consort with them.

Don't come home with a bargain-basement collar and try to buckle that around Capricorn cat's neck. Select an expensive genuine leather one studded with jewels (real ones from Tiffany's would be nice) that compliments his coloring. A cheap basket with a discarded old sweater or petticoat tossed in for a blanket will be an outrageous insult to his social standing. He wants a handmade imported blanket woven in

Spain or Italy folded neatly in a handcrafted basket designed especially to tally with his measurements.

Nothing would delight him more than having Santa Claus put a sterling silver bowl (with his name engraved in elegant script) under the Christmas tree for him.

Because a Capricorn native is impressed with social status, he is concerned with the "who" as well as the "what" of the persons he associates with. He is just a shade under being a la-di-da snobcat.

Less romantically inclined than a Scorpio or Leo cat, your cat will check the pedigree, address, age, color, and disposition of any prospective partner. When one has passed inspection, your cat will take time setting the stage for seduction.

"Lovemaking is serious business, so I won't rush into this. if I've decided that gorgeous creature is acceptable, there's no question about capitulation the moment I make my first advances and my superiority is instantly recognized."

This cat does not demand much attention, so people can come and go without realizing how cat-managed you and your home are. You do not need to reassure him constantly that he is Mr. Terrific, either. He knows he is, which is sufficient.

Anything or anybody with snob appeal will appeal to your cat; so he will be on hand to check out your guests to see whether they are socially respectable and to study their manners to determine whether they have memorized Emily Post. As long as his routine is not disturbed and his toys and possessions are left untouched, he will tolerate your guests—if they pass his standards, that is, and they behave according to the rules of etiquette.

Outwardly cooperative, a Capricorn cat is still persistent as all natives of an earth sign are; so he will not run the risk of being swatted with a newspaper if he uses your best chair for a scratching post. He will use it, of course, but not when you are around. He is not going to tolerate your lack of attention to keeping his litter pan spotless. He may punish you if you are neglectful by using the corner behind the sofa, which will offend his sensibilities almost as much as yours. But training a human is important, so it may require a small sacrifice now and then that may be distasteful but highly effective.

Because he is so addicted to correct conduct, he will be the devoted companion he believes a cat should be when the human who cared for him when he was young becomes old.

He would serve you meals in bed if you were sick (if he could), and he will stay faithfully close to you when you are downhearted. He will never notice your gray hairs, or if he does he will consider them proper and becoming to an older person.

Once you have won his love, he will never become the cranky and grumpy old sourpuss he could become if he is not given the proper respect and attention. He will give you love as generously as you give it to him—provided, of course, that it is bestowed on him in the peaceful and well-ordered environment his proper little soul requires. Actually, he is so well-behaved and respectable that he is the Mr. Somebody he says he is.

COMPATIBLE SIGNS: Capricorn, Taurus, Cancer, Virgo, Pisces, and Libra natives will fall into line without too much coaching and gain the approval of this cat, who is a worshiper at the altar of proper behavior.

LESS-COMPATIBLE SIGNS: Aries, Gemini, Leo, Scorpio, Sagittarius, and Aquarius humans will be apt to drive this cat to nervous prostration. If one of these Sun signs is yours, you will need to toe the mark sooner or later—and it had better be sooner. When you have shaped up, your little snobbish cat will make you proud of the way you think you have shaped him up.

Aquarius the Water Bearer

(January 21 through February 19

What's so great about goldfish in a bowl?
I'll tell you. It's because they zoom
Around like crazy when I'm sloshing up
The water.
What's so great about the toilet bowl?
Yoweee. It's a typhoon in there when
Someone trips the lever.
And, man, is it fun to
Stick my feet into that whirlpool.
What's so great about rain puddles?
Zounds! They're fun to splash through.
That's why.
Any more dumb questions you want answers to?

The *Aquarius* Cat

Born under the influence of Uranus, your Aquarian cat was born with a figurative caul over its face. He is a mystery, and he will remain one all the days of his life. He may stand on his head as often as his feet trying to find the answer to a multitude of puzzles.

Born in the autumn of the zodiac, he was astrologically advanced in wisdom as an infant, and he keeps getting wiser as he grows bigger. Woven from the strands of the enigmatic Uranus, your cat defies cataloging. So do not ever expect to drop him in a file marked "Understood," for he will never fit that evaluation.

He is such a bundle of paradoxes; he is a quivering bunch of conflicting emotions. He is timid and moves with caution. His mind is so filled with ideas and a number of things that he has difficulty keeping them organized. Even when he has no idea where he is going, he has plenty of ideas about how to get there and what to do when he does.

Sweet and pliable though he may appear, he is still stubborn and determined. His first reaction to anything you suggest will be a stouthearted *Meow.* Translation: *No!*

It is not that he is defiant or contrary, it is just that he wants to be absolutely sure he wants to do what you want him to do. Suggest a walk through the park, and he will think, "Now, that sounds amusing, then again it could be a deadly bore. I'll have to give that proposition more thought." If you really want him to go with you, try putting some coaxing sweet talk in his ears. That will usually persuade him.

This is a cat who is torn between wanting to be caught up in a social whirl (yours will do nicely if he can't generate his own) and needing a great deal of peace and routine. He is sensitive and emotional; so activity drains his energy and yet it is difficult for him to resist the temptations that propel him into either physical or mental activity. His fixed air sign means that he is like the air—here, there, everywhere. Actually, though, he is not as interested in taking his body somewhere as he is going there in his mind. Less effort, you understand.

Although all cats have mysterious eyes, his are filled with a dreamy look that means he is on a trip to some never-never world of his own on earth or some other planet. He would be right at home living with Alice behind the looking glass, for the topsy-turvy world created by Aquarian Lewis Carroll would seem completely right-side-up to your cat. If you could peer into his mind, you would think you were invading the thoughts of Walter Mitty.

When your cat is sitting with his eyes focused on something that is not there (as far as you can see), he is seeing something that is there. He may visualize himself sitting on the topmost branch of that oak tree, trying to catch the rainbow tangled in its branches; he may be dressed in knee-high red boots and a green hat with a purple plume carrying his sword to the White House as a gift for the president; he may be smacking his lips over that blackbird pie he sees you baking for him; or he may be handling the controls of a space capsule as the head astronaut going to the moon—or better yet to Uranus.

Because he is so fascinated with new ideas and experiences, he forgets sometimes that his body is attached to that active mind, and he may do some pretty dumb things. Like, for instance, plopping his paws down on top of the hot toaster to get a better look at the cardinal sitting on the bird feeder. Or jumping into the bathtub when it is half full of water because he thought that floating bar of soap was a real live baby duck.

He is not a hunter or a fighter, for he loves all things great and small (even humans). And while he is very loving, he is less interested in romance than a Leo or Scorpio or Aries. So your February valentine cat isn't going to get all goose-pimply over the 14th or be out every night hunting up amorous paramours. In fact, he may be so long waking up to the fact that cats do some mighty interesting things together that you may begin to wonder whether he is normal. Don't worry, he is. But he will spend more time thinking about sex than indulging in it. And when he does begin looking around, he will be almost as fastidious as the Capricorn cat down the avenue.

Although he would be happy living in Wonderland, he is

139

at home in the world of reality, too. He analyzes as well as fantasises, and he is able to make you feel like a bug being dissected by a gimlet-eyed scientist when he fixes you with a disapproving stare if you do something even slightly dishonest.

He considers you guilty of hypocrisy if you tell the salesman at the door you are just leaving for the dentist's office when he just saw you popping a cake into the oven. If you chortle over some guest who comes to the door whom he knows you can't tolerate, he is going to be most disapproving. He is not quite as critical as a Virgo cat or as intolerant as the Capricorn feline, but he is no happy-go-lucky Sagittarian, either.

Because his sign is symbolized by the water bearer, you should not be surprised to see him splashing through puddles with his face tipped up to catch the raindrops when sane and rational cats are snoozing before the fire. He is going to infuriate you when he tips over the fishbowl because he has all four paws in it, or stands on the toilet seat dipping water out of it (or, worse, trying to drink it). But shocking you is something that tickles him; so be shocked if you want him beaming with delight over his own zaniness.

A conventional approach to anything is dreary and dull. Unlike the Virgo cat who suffers agonies when his dish is not set squarely on the same spot every day, your little cuckoo may want to eat his supper on the fireplace mantel or on top of a stack of records going round and round on the turntable. He may decide that sleeping on top of the refrigerator is more conducive to fruitcake dreams than napping on his own bed.

He is not a coward, but he is no warrior, either. So when things begin to get rough and tough where the catboys gather, he will simply wave goodbye and flip his tail in farewell as he strolls home. He is not one to lurk in the shadows waiting for anything. There is too much chance it might be dangerous.

Paradoxical as he is, he will want to do everything contrary to what normal cats do. For instance, when other cats are checking in for breakfast, he will want out to check on the hornets' nest to see whether those buzzing inhabitants are up yet. When other cats are settling down for a long winter's nap, he will be yowling to get out and tromp in the snow.

The time of day, the season, the month, the year are of no interest. He is an advocate of the here-and-now philosophy. What intrigues him at the moment is all that matters.

Of course, your friends refer to him as Your Crazy Cat, but neither you nor your cat really care too much what they think. He is so carefree wandering through his land of magic and fantasy and thinking up new ways to do old things that he will fascinate you every day.

He will not make demands on you. If you are there when he needs his wet paws wiped off, his blanket fluffed up at bedtime, and his meals served more or less on time he will be satisfied. The rest of his affairs he can manage quite well by himself, thank you, and if something really does puzzle him he will find the solution somewhere in his inventive mind. Even if it is a perfectly ridiculous one.

Susceptible to anemia, blood poisoning, and circulatory ailments, you will need to be on guard to detect some disorder before it becomes serious. It is unlikely, however, that he

 141

will slink away to suffer alone, for he is too eager to be up and at 'em to endure discomfort longer than necessary. You will be given the message when he needs medical help.

COMPATIBLE SIGNS: Aquarians will find this Merry-Andrew cat a fascinating performer. His craziness and bizarre behavior will enchant you because you are something like that yourself, you know. And your cat will think he has been transported to Storybook Land because you are so indulgent and permissive. The two of you will have a storybook life together.

LESS-COMPATIBLE SIGNS: Gemini, Leo, Libra, Sagittarius, or Pisces humans may find his bang-bang approach to things too frazzling to the nerves. But if they can adapt to his ludicrous behavior and his unorthodox lifestyle they should make it together.

NON-COMPATIBLE SIGN: An Aries, Taurus, Cancer, Virgo, Scorpio, or Capricorn will find the adrenalin pumping overtime and hair turning gray (if it doesn't fall out) trying to cope with this adventurer from Wonderland. But if you can look the other way and not interfere or criticize his unconventional behavior, you can adjust—in time. It is going to be hard to ignore him; so you will have to adapt. And when you do, you will find your life will be shaken up delightfully.

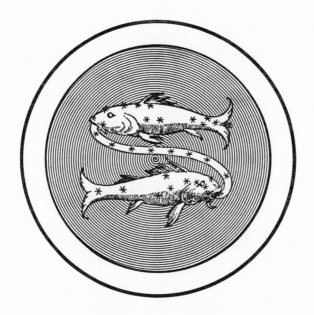

Pisces the Fish

(February 20 through March 20th)

Life is such a bafflement sometimes.
And you are, too. When you keep asking me
Why I'm staring into space.
Why shouldn't I stare into space?
I see lots of things that aren't there
For you to see. They are things only a cat
Like me can see and understand.
And that's because I am very unique.
And I'm classified as E.S.F.
What's E.S.F.? *Extra Special Feline.*
How dense you humans are sometimes.

The *Pisces* Cat

Born under the influence of Neptune (God of the Waters) your Piscean cat is so mysterious that trying to categorize him is comparable to shoveling fog with a snow shovel. When it was said that the cat appeared as if by magic some 4,000 years ago as a full-blown enigmatic package, it was probably being said about a Pisces cat.

This Sun sign, the last of the 12 in the zodiac, symbolizes completeness. If Aries is the astrological infant of the universe, then Pisces is the old soul possessing all the mystical qualities of having learned all there is to know about all there is—and remembering it, if not consciously—then unconsciously.

A Neptunian knows intuitively far more than he knows he knows, for his sign denotes spiritual development and an awareness of mystical and spiritual things. It is also a water sign making the natives extremely emotional and sensitive who relate to their environment with hearts rather than minds. And this could be (often is) their undoing.

The symbol of two fish swimming in opposite directions means that a Neptunian can rise to the heights or sink to the depths depending on the goals he sets for himself and the controls he places on his behavior.

Piscean kittens are born looking so angelic that they seem to have floated down from some sugarplum tree in Fairytale Land where they consorted with elves and pixies and socialized with angels. They are so gentle and docile, they seem almost too good to be true. And they will remain that way all through life unless they are misunderstood and mistreated. If they are mishandled, they become neurotic and withdrawn.

If your cat is typical, he is delicate and dainty with fine silky hair. And he probably has the most luminous and entrancing eyes ever seen in any cat. Like limpid pools, they are filled with strange lights that seem to reflect the memories of a never-never world where he once lived, a world where he might have played with moonbeams, caught stardust in his paws, and wound rainbow strands around his neck. A world where he knew the sea, where he talked with the fish, and heard the songs of mermaids in conch shells.

The rhythm of the sea is the music his drummer plays and what he hears when he dreams of (or remembers) a tranquil and serene world where fish swim gracefully through their vivid yet silent world. A Neptunian cat would be delirious living by the sea, where he could sit on the rocks watching the tides come and go and gazing far into the horizon behind which is the land of make-believe that to him is reality.

148

There seems to be a mysterious aura surrounding your cat that proects him from the harsh reality of That World Out There where bad boys tie tin cans to kittens' tails and bully cats threaten shy and peace-loving creatures. Your cat would prefer meandering through fields of clover to slinking through weeds stalking birds or mice. He is blissful just watching the bees and butterflies without considering how it would be to catch one. And if he could watch and listen to the music of Mantovani violins, he would be transported to a celestial paradise.

Like the Aquarian cat, he is oblivious to routine and schedules, for they threaten his tranquility and are things that make his dreamworld impossible to inhabit. But rather than fight them, he ignores them. And he succeeds in thwarting them through passive resistance rather than overt warfare.

Night and day are one and the same to him. He may sleep one night curled up on the foot of your bed and stay up the next night wandering through the house watching the shadows on the carpet made by the moon peeking through the willow tree.

He may eat one day and forget all about food the next. Or if he does think about it he may not recall where his bowl of kibbles might be. Some nights he may decide at 2 A.M. that it is an ideal time for a snack. He will rout you out of bed and pipe you to the kitchen almost singing his lilting meows. Before you are aware of what is happening, you will find yourself shoving a can of tuna through the can opener. He will charm you with his gentle persuasion instead of bossing you around with howls and yowls. He will climb on your pillow and tickle your eyelids with his whiskers while he purrs in your ear, and you may grumble and groan but whatever he is asking for he will get.

His vagueness may disconcert you unless you understand that it is only because he is so involved with his dreams that the world of reality ceases to exist. When that happens, remember that he has a sense of humor and he delights in seeing humans act nutty. So you can hold his attention by being a clown. Try standing on your head and making faces at him or dancing the cha-cha around his bowl of chow when he won't eat. He may become so fascinated and bemused by your performance that he might demolish the stuff without even knowing what he was doing.

Because he is so undemanding and out of touch with reality much of the time, it is easy to overlook him and forget to give him the love and attention he needs. He needs to be praised for being good. For he is good, very, very good. And when your whispered sweet nothings flow into his ears, they are as soothing to his sentimental soul as the music of the sea would be.

He is so beguiled by the offbeat behavior of an unconventional human that he would be giggly being dressed up in a cape and bonnet and wheeled to the supermarket in a doll buggy. He would not consider it at all eccentric to carry on conversations with you that would cause a rational being to lift his eyebrows and make circles with a finger pointed toward his head.

Whispered questions like, "Hey, did you know there's a pixie hiding behind that vase?" would delight him. Or saying, "I think the man in the moon is looking at us, and I do believe he's waving to you," would make sense to him. It might make sense to you, too, if you were told that he had been talking to that pixie a few minutes ago, and that the man in the moon was indeed waving to him because he had once been acquainted with your Neptunian cat.

Cats endowed with unusual grace and litheness are probably natives of this Sun sign, for your cat can weave his way though the bric-a-brac on the whatnot shelves with the fluidity of water flowing around a rock. When he is up there hunting for that fairy he thought he saw behind the cranberry glass vase, just relax. Remember the fish? Your cat will flow around obstacles with the same ease that a fish swims around a coral reef or through a tangle of seaweed.

Like a Cancer cat, your cat is extremely sensitive to criticism—real or suspected—and he will be wounded to the core of his tender heart if there is the slightest injury to his feelings. Anyone who has studied feline behavior knows that some cats are far more easily offended than others. Criticism, scoldings, punishments, neglect will only drive your cat deeper into his dream world of fantasy and make him fearful of everything and everyone—perhaps even you.

A Neptunian kitten's godmother is kind when she places it in a situation where there is no restriction on drifting through a fantasy world. Being compelled to cope with the harsh world of reality of rubbish heaps, snarling dogs, cruel people, roaring motor vehicles would drive a cat like this to the brink of insanity—probably right over it.

Then, too, a Pisces cat's vitality is almost as fragile as his inability to withstand confusion and threatening dangers. As a result, he is highly susceptible to illnesses, some of which may be located in the throat, lungs, and intestinal tract.

Togetherness is the code he lives by, which means he will cling to you for security and protection. His clingingness and devotion are so disarming that he has no need of weapons of any kind. Without fighting a single battle for control over you and his environment, he will win the war (if one is declared). But you will be the declarer—not he—for he would not recognize a warrior if he saw one, let alone be one.

And he is not much of a philanderer, either, for he is too engrossed in his dream world to be overly concerned with lovemaking which usually leads to responsibilities that demand time and attention—like kittens who require dutiful care by a doting parent.

Understand from the very start that you are involved with an old soul who may have traveled many roads through many incarnations to find you. And that he has come to comfort you. When you sit by the fire dreaming of your yesteryears and how it was, he will be sitting right there by your side (or on your lap) in companionable silence remembering, too, how it was once in a vaguely remembered fairytale land.

COMPATIBLE SIGNS: Probably the happiest created-in-heaven combination would be putting two Pisces natives together. Both of you would be dreamers dreaming together. And you would adore one another. As long as only one of you has to deal with reality and keep a roof over both your heads (which is you, of course), enough stability would exist to keep two Pisceans from floating away into a world of fantasy.

A Taurus, Cancer, Capricorn, or Aquarius person would enjoy the togetherness a Pisces cat craves and must have. Your own homeloving tendencies would help stabilize your cat's environment. And you have enough sentimental and romantic tendencies yourself to give you an understanding of this mystifying cat.

LESS-COMPATIBLE SIGNS: If you are an Aries, Gemini, Leo, Virgo, Libra, Scorpio, or Sagittarian you are going to have to face the fact that your cat is not an explosive firecracker with lots of spunk and gutsy behavior. But the sweetness and otherworldliness of your cat may be exactly what you need to remind you that magic, fantasy, mystery, poetry, music, and romance can be shields to protect you from the blows you take in the world of reality.

Afterword

Naturally, you turned first to the chapter that discusses your cat's Sun sign. And you may have said, "Now, if that isn't the silliest thing I ever read. My cat isn't one speck like that description. It's obvious that astrology can't be applied to cats!"

Just a minute. Before you toss the book into the trash bin, call your cat over and read the section on his Sun sign out loud so he can hear it. Then ask him what he thinks about it. You are positive that he will agree with you that it is downright silly? You are? All right, call him over and let's hear what he says.

"Well, now," says he, "that's as accurate a description of what I'm like as I've ever heard. If you don't agree with me, then it's because your treatment of me doesn't correlate with my personality.

"The thing wrong with you is that you've thought of me as just a cat like all other cats. And that's where you've not used intelligence. Of course, I know all about Sun signs and astrology. And I know how I was influenced by my Sun sign when I came into this incarnation, but you've never paid any attention to that. I'm glad someone has finally opened your eyes and made you see how astrology does affect all creatures—even you and me."

People who have not had the joy of living with many cats have been denied the pleasure of learning that they do indeed have unique personalities, just as we humans do. How would you like it if you were tossed into a barrel labeled, "Humans. They're all alike. Take your choice."

Well, cats are all alike only in that they all have four legs, a head and a tail (as a rule) just as humans are all alike in that they all have two legs, one head, and no tail. But that's where the similarity ends.

So give your cat a chance to be what he was ordained to be by showing him a new understanding of his uniqueness. And then let him be what his Sun sign made him be. You have nothing to lose and a whole lot to gain.

Viewing your cat through astrologically adjusted eyes will give you a new insight into his innermost thoughts and feelings. And when you understand him better, you will treat him better. And that will make him happier living with you. Whether you are happier living with him is of no concern whatsoever. It is his happiness we are concerned with—not yours.